FALMOUTH'S WARTIME MEMORIES

A series of personal

recollections

as told to

Trelawny

and published to

commemorate the fiftieth

anniversary of D-Day June 6 1944

British National Bibliographical Cataloguing

Falmouth's Wartime Memories

© Arwenack Press - 1994

ISBN 1 899121 00 5

Published in Great Britain 1994

All rights reserved. No part of this publication may be reproduced or transmitted in any form or by any means, electronic or mechanical, including photocopying, recording, or any information storage and retrieval system, without permission in writing from the copyright holder and publisher

Printed and published by Arwenack Press
Tregoniggie Industrial Estate
Falmouth, Cornwall TR11 4SN

CONTENTS

PAGE

6	Preface
7	Falmouth Commemorative week 13th-19th June 1994
9	Ships set on fire in docks
11	The *Schleswig Holstein's* visit
12	We watched the formation of the British Expeditionary Force
15	By tug to Dunkirk beaches
21	Diary records dramatic days in June 1940
24	Front line Falmouth-1940
27	Falmouth defends itself for Second World War
31	Dutch navy remembers those war years at Enys
35	Good friends from Holland
37	Dutch sisters' enquiry
38	Castle guns fired once in anger
40	Memories of Dad's Army
46	On guard in 1940 against Hitler's Hordes
50	German View of Falmouth
52	Falmouth's first air raid
55	A bomb cut our home in half
60	When bombs fell on Falmouth
66	A raid moulded this man's life
67	Huddled under the stairs when the bombs fell
69	Fuel tanks bombed
71	A Lucky Shot that saved the docks
73	An explosion like a huge steam hammer hitting buildings
76	Divers search for traces of 1941 tragedy
80	Falmouth rescue and decontamination squad
81	'If invasion comes then blow up the docks'
83	Preparations for D-Day
87	A few hours of isolation cooled hot tempers
91	Floating tables with four legs
92	Building the Mulberry Harbours
94	Bitter sweet memories for the W.R.N.S.
96	The role of Falmouth's hotels in wartime
99	The greatest raid of all
101	From the Penryn river they sailed to glory
103	Where MLs were prepared for the St. Nazaire raid
105	Eight men returned—as corpses
107	A family link with America
111	Trebah's place in history

PAGE

113 Servicemen return to Japanese attack scene
115 'Small cog' with such a vital wartime role
117 The day we drove over an unexploded bomb
120 From £9 car to fire engine
121 A link first forged in the War
123 Another who missed death in *Lancastria*
124 Merchant Navy Pool memories
125 Swanvale fuel tanks hit by raiders
126 A dockworker in two world wars
127 Veterans' association prepares for D-Day anniversary events
129 How the town remembered those who went to war
132 Miracle Escape
133 Convoy Commodore once captain of *Ganges*
135 Yanks come back
137 From the roar of aircraft engines to the peace of the Helford
140 Falmouth and the Victoria Cross awards
142 Captured by the Nazis
144 Attempt to solve a wartime mystery
145 A tragic accident
146 Russian Convoy memories
148 Zeppelin raids
150 Runners were sent on secret sea missions
151 More on the MGBs
152 Sir George and the runners
153 Torpedoed off The Lizard
155 Local wartime craft
157 How the *Q9* sank four U boats
160 Thanks to the *MBM*
162 Bombed and strafed by the Germans
164 Young evacuees afraid to walk in the woods
166 Famous visitors
167 Lt Cdr Robert Hichens

LIST OF ILLUSTRATIONS

8	An American Liberty ship and salvage tug in docks
10	Falmouth "A" group section wardens
11	The Battleship *Schleswig Holstein* visiting Falmouth in 1939
12	Group of Falmouth Territorials (Royal Artillery) 1939
13	Falmouth Territorial Army members in a Devonport barracks
15	Lieut. Percy Mark Johns, RNVR
21	Bordeaux refugees at Falmouth
34	RAF barrage ballon site on The Beacon
40	Home Guard parade on The Moor
42	Penryn Home Guard
43	Members of the Home guard take part in the exercise "Stand Easy"
50	German aerial photograph of Falmouth
55	Falmouth ARP Wardens
56	Air raid 30 May 1944—Melvill Crescent
57	Air raid 30 May 1944—shelter which saved 26 persons
59	An unexploded bomd in Marlborough Avenue
60	Trevethan School after bombing
61	Church Service on The Moor
62	Train bombed in cutting near Falmouth
68	Philip Lee Bishop with the bulldozer he used at Swanvalw
71	The King and Queen at Falmouth Docks 1942
79	An unexploded landmine
80	Falmouth Rescue and Decontamination Squad 1945
81	Falmouth Industrial Bomb Disposal Squad—July 1945
83	Invasion craft at the Empire Jetty—1944
85	Invasion craft in dry dock
86	US landing craft at Grove Place in 1943
90	Mulberry harbour sections at the docks
92	Landing Craft on Trebah beach
95	HM The Queen inspecting WRNS at Falmouth
96	Boscawen and Pentargan Hotels bombed on 30 May 1944
99	*HMS Campbeltown* rammed into the dock gate at St. Nazaire
100	A damaged LCT in dry dock
104	A 'Wings for Victory' gathering outside the Town Hall on The moor
107	David Clarke—adopted as mascot by the Yanks
108	The Americans towing Bofors gun, Red Lion, Mawnan Smith
108	Entrance to USA AAB on The Beacon
109	US Base on The Beacon
119	Artists impression of the harbour in 1944 by Tony Warren
122	VE -Day Street Party- Berkeley Cottages
129	The Falmouth Tribute Fund booklet and tankard
130	The dedication of the sea-front shelter
133	Outward bound convoy No. 330
134	American troops at Market Strand during exercise "Duck"
147	US troops being fed during exercise "Duck"
149	LCT loaded withvehicles leaving the old submarine pier
150	*Gay Viking*
161	The World War 1 "Q" ship *Mary B Mitchell*
163	Bomb disposal squad loading an unexploded bom into their lorry
167	Lt Cdr Robert Hichens

Preface

At 15 minutes past midnight on June 6 1944, Operation Overlord, the Allied invasion of Europe began. Since then, that day has been known as D-Day.

At that time there were 15,000 American troops in Cornwall, many members of the 29th U.S. Infantry Division which had come to the UK in 1942, plus troops from other parts of Britain.

This influx of American troops had a major impact on the county. Many country roads leading to specially built 'hards' for landing craft were widened and re-metalled. There are people who remember, as children, their wide-eyed amazement at seeing coloured humans for the first time, and being warned by parents "Behave yourself or the black man will get you!" But lasting friendships were forged in those stirring times. A number of GI brides came from Cornwall.

A shelter on Falmouth's sea front was given to the town by the 'Yanks' in appreciation of the welcome they had received, and from our shores thousands of allied troops embarked for the invasion beaches in Normandy, bearing the names Utah, Omaha, Gold, Juno and Sword.

During the last eight years Trelawny has interviewed many residents in and around Falmouth for his nostalgic page, published first in the 'Leader' then the 'West Briton'. Inevitably many of those people had vivid wartime experiences to recall. These have now been extracted, and are reproduced in this book - a unique record of Falmouth's War Memories from Dunkirk to 'D' day.

The Second World War from 1939 to 1945 was an eventful time for Falmouth. Probably because of its strategic and geographical position, set at the entrance to the Western Approaches, with a fine dockyard, ship repair facilities and and third finest natural harbour in the world, it was continually involved, from Dunkirk to D-Day. For the latter event the Americans were here and from rivers and creeks around the port the landing craft were assembled and serviced. In 1942 the raid on St Nazaire - described as "the greatest raid of all"- was mounted from Falmouth.

The Germans, too, realised Falmouth's importance. It has been claimed that the town had more air raid alerts than any other community in the country, but bombs did fall and ships were hit and residents died.

The author expresses gratitude to Northcliffe Newspapers and Cornish Newspapers Ltd for granting permission for these articles to be reproduced.

The month and year in which each article first appeared is included with each extract.

The majority of pictures in this book have been supplied by Mr Peter Gilson of the Falmouth History Research Group of the Royal Cornwall Polytechnic Society to whom grateful thanks are extended. These, and many other pictures from the past, can be inspected, by appointment, and can be seen in the Polytechnic Society's building in Church Street, Falmouth.

Included also are a number of extracts from Mr. Bernard Breakell's informative book "Falmouth at War".

Readers may disagree with some of the facts mentioned, but it must be emphasised the memories recounted here have been recalled after a lapse of half a century. While the experiences remain vivid, the very passage of time has convinced those interviewed that the details given by them must be accurate.

Falmouth Commemorative Week 13th-19th June 1994

MONDAY 13th JUNE - CIVIC RECEPTION
Invited Veterans to attend a Civic Reception in Falmouth Arts Centre - screening of archive film

TUESDAY 14th JUNE - A NIGHT AT THE 'FLICKS' FALMOUTH ARTS CENTRE
Relive the era through film. Handpicked for the occasion

WEDNESDAY 15th JUNE - BEACH BARBECUE AT TOLVERNE (SMUGGLERS COTTAGE)
One of the **three D-Day embarkation points** in the area.

THURSDAY 16th JUNE - WORLD WAR II SHOW, PRINCESS PAVILION, FALMOUTH
8 p.m. A full evening's authentic entertainment with live music from **Peter Pathfinder's Trio** and a cabaret spot from their very own "forces sweetheart" Natalie Ellis

FRIDAY 17th JUNE - 'A TRIBUTE TO THE 40s', PRINCESS PAVILION, FALMOUTH
8 p.m. The **Johnny Austen Show Band** play music of the era

SATURDAY 18th JUNE 10 a.m. - DISPLAY OF MILITARY VEHICLES, PENDENNIS CASTLE, FALMOUTH
8 p.m. - Princess Pavilion - Dancing to the music of the 40s with **Roger Polmear**

SUNDAY 19th JUNE - COMMEMORATIVE SERVICE 11 a.m.
In Falmouth's Parish Church - **King Charles the Martyr** - Parade from Webber Street, through the town centre to the Church led by the band of the Royal Marines.
Sunday Afternoon
Porthleven Town Band in Gyllyngdune Gardens, Falmouth

Sunday Evening - 8 p.m. PRINCESS PAVILION
St Stythians Band play 'Sounds of the 40s'

FRIDAY 17th JUNE - TUESDAY 21st JUNE - *S.S. JOHN W BROWN*
The Libery Ship S.S. John W Brown *will be visiting Falmouth as part of her commemoration tour. She was built in 41 days in Baltimore and was designed to last just a few voyages—as were her 2700 sister ships! This fine old ship has been renovated by a team of volunteers and is now one of only three intact Libertys remaining from the great fleet. The* John W Brown *will be alongside in Falmouth Docks during the above period*

FRIDAY 17th JUNE - SUNDAY 18th JUNE - ROYAL NETHERLANDS NAVY
The Royal Netherlands navy have made available several mine hunters and they will be in Falmouth Docks during the above dates. The Dutch presence in Falmouth during the lead-up to D-Day was considerable

OTHER EVENTS

A series of exhibitions will be mounted at various venues throughout the County from late may onwards. These will depict 'Cornwall at War' and will be themed according to the venues' locations.

An American Liberty ship and salvage tug in the docks

8

SHIPS SET ON FIRE IN DOCKS

The picture on the cover depicts what was probably the most severe raid of the Second World War on Falmouth docks. One beautiful day in the summer of 1942 two planes approached from the North West, coming in over Mabe and Penryn. They tore over the harbour, releasing their bombs and made away over the Bay. There were no barrage balloons up at that time and the guns only started firing after they had made their swoop.

Part of one stick of bombs fell on Trefusis field leaving craters which were visible long after the war had ended. But they hit the *Tiara*, a brand new Anglo Saxon Petroleum Company tanker on the Northern arm setting her alight. The tanker *British Chancellor* next to her was set on fire and sank. The next vessel, the *Tuscalusa* was also left burning as was the *Marie Chandris* of the Chandris Line, loaded with cotton. This ship burned for six days and nights.

At that time Mr. Gordon Martin, now a retired tug skipper, was mate of the tug *Fernleigh*. She was undergoing a refit and he was acting as coxswain of the Towage Company's launch, in which he was instructed to take electricians to the hospital ship *Atlantis* laid up in the Fal. With him was Mr. Cedric Thomas. They were off Penarrow Point when the bombs fell. When they returned to the harbour a column of thick black smoke was rising from the burning ships by the Northern arm. Four vessels there had been hit.

At the end of the Northern arm 50 to 100 men were trapped in a concrete section where they had run for shelter. Most were dock workers and many were badly burnt. Gordon, his father in his boat and another launch rescued these men. He paid tribute to 'Gipsy' Daniels, a member of the tank cleaning gang, who helped many of the injured men to safety and said Mr. Martin "did a wonderful job there at the end of the Northern breakwater."

Marie Chandris was later towed from inside the Northern to the back of the Eastern breakwater, where she was grounded, while the firemen were trying to put out the flames.

Two days later on high water she was towed to a site off St. Mawes where she was put inside the Lugo buoy, grounded and sunk. While there she burned for yet another day. She was finally broken up by Sawle Bros., scrap merchants.

Tiara was pulled clear by the tugs and boarded by pilot Jackson, who helped release the hawsers holding her, and for his brave action he received an award.

There were a number of casualties in all the ships involved.

Another nautical disaster of those war years involving Falmouth was when the 15,000 ton general cargo ship *Registan*, operating as a merchant raider came into the bay badly damaged after encountering a German raider in the Western Approaches. Harbour tugs towed her alongside. She was armed fore and aft. Her bulkheads had exploded and oil tanks caught fire literally frying many of the crew members in the oil.

On this occasion too "Gipsy" Daniels and his tank cleaning colleagues did sterling work recovering the bodies. The ship was eventually repaired and one of her cutters was presented to Falmouth Sea Cadet Corps by the Royal Navy in recognition of the help received in Falmouth. Mr. Gordon Martin was the CPO instructor to the Corps at that time.

Falmouth "A" Group section wardens

The *Schleswig Holstein's* visit

VISITING a friend in West Cornwall last weekend I was reminded of an event in Falmouth's pre-war shipping history.

It was in early summer 1939 that the German battleship *Schleswig Holstein* paid a courtesy call to the port. She was one of the few foreign battleships ever permitted to anchor in St. Just pool.

The battleship was full of cadets - all hand picked Aryan types. Few

The German battleship Schleswig Holstein *visiting Falmouth in 1939*

were under six feet tall, all had blond hair and their uniforms were of the finest texture.

Looking back, it was a typical Goebbels Nazi-type propaganda exercise. These young Germans exuded friendliness. Townsfolk were invited on board and I vividly recall seeing on the wardroom wall pictures of Stukas divebombing and a big picture of Adolf Hitler.

The cadets took innumerable pictures. One Falmothian recalled seeing a group at Treluswell cross, taking photographs. I wonder how many of these prints were consulted when the port was later bombed!

Then *Schleswig Holstein* left - to the strains of a band playing on Pendennis Point, where a big crowd had gathered to wave farewell.

How ironic that just a few weeks later this vessel fired the first shots of the Second World War in Poland.

April 18, 1987

We watched the formation of the British Expeditionary Force

We've heard so much about it recently—the outbreak of World War II exactly fifty years ago.

Some old friends and I were reminiscing recently about those days when one of them asked me how I, as a member of the Territorial Army, had fared. He added that I had never spoken about those early days.

On a Thursday in July the TA was embodied and as members of the 56 HAA Regiment we climbed that evening into the backs of lorries in

Group of Falmouth Territorials (Royal Artillery) 1939. About to entrain at Falmouth Station Left to right: "Stinker" Pugh, Frank Bennetts, Bernard "Berbie"Hughes, Maurice "Morrie" Osborne, Denzil "Grub" Rundle, Phil "Splits" Belletti, Roy "Porker" Johns, Freddie Truscott.

the yard of the Barracks at the end of Grove Place and to waves from crowds of relatives and friends who had gathered there we drove off up Avenue Road, Melvill Road and out of town making for Devonport where we occupied a part of Raglan Barracks.

Grey, sprawling, dirty and forbidding and surrounded by high stone walls and ugly iron railings, this proved anything but a cheerful spot.

A friend thought it looked like a Foreign Legion outpost with its huge parade square faced by tall mesh-covered windows. It had been derelict since the Great War, occupied only occasionally by tramps.

We had to dig out the toilets and move five or six inches of rubble from the floors of rooms before they were habitable.

We slept on the floor covered with blankets, with 'tables, six foot' the only furnishing.

Another friend who had been a trainee in the Borough Sanitary Inspector's office, had the unenviable responsibility for the removal of swill and the cleanliness of dustbins.

Then on September 3rd I recall I was in the area between the tall outer wall and a barrack block when over a radio speaker I heard

Falmouth Territorial Army members enjoy a sing-song in a Devonport barracks shortly after embodiment.

Premier Neville Chamberlain tell us there had been no reply to our ultimatum and Britain was again at war with Germany. We heard this without emotion. It had seemed obvious it was coming. At least we now knew where we stood. That night the air raid sirens sounded over Plymouth. Apparently Sunderland flying boats were flying and someone was taking no chances.

During the following weeks day followed monotonous day, broken only by visits to Plymouth and walks along Union Street, by now full of naval and Army personnel. But into the barracks each day came a crocodile of civilians—smart and shabby—who were speedily issued with uniforms. Before long the whole vast barrack square was full of squads being drilled. After only six or seven weeks these same men marched smartly out—converted into soldiers.

We were, in fact, watching the birth of part of the British Expeditionary Force that was later to be evacuated from Dunkirk. Finally, shortly after Christmas, our group at Regimental HQ was broken up and we moved to Barracks in Crownhill where we joined a section of the 165 Heavy Anti Aircraft Battery—largely made up of men from Camborne and Redruth. For our Falmouth group the war had really started. Not long after some of us manned an anti-aircraft gun in a field at Ernesettle overlooking the Tamar, and gazed with longing at trains crossing the Brunel bridge back into Cornwall.

October 14, 1989

By tug to Dunkirk beaches

It was a beautiful day in May 1940, and we were doing our best to enjoy it. Gyllyngvase Beach at Falmouth is a very pleasant place to be when summer arrives early, and you are "standing by" with little to do but await instructions which will send you to replace the next engineer officer who falls ill in one of His Majesty's Ships.

One might almost have forgotten the war on this day, and as we bathed and frollicked in the blazing sunshine the charms of this section of the Cornish Riviera almost obliterated the events which were taking place on the other side of that strip of Mediterranean blue water. Almost, but not quite. Only too well did we realise the agony and trial of the British Expeditionary Force, which now, brave but battered, fought its stubborn way back and ever back through a capitulated France in the face of the advancing Nazi hordes.

Lieut. Percy Mark Johns, RNVR

As we stared out to sea through the barbed-wire monstrosities which now, of necessity, defaced the natural beauty of the promenade, we wondered how many gallant British soldiers were at that moment fighting for their lives across the water.

Our thoughts were rudely interrupted by the arrival of a miniature cyclone in the shape of a breathless, panting Wren from the Naval Base. She and two others, so she informed us, had been sent out with instructions to find me at all costs, and had eventually located me after trying all the usual haunts of temporary idle Naval personnel. The naval signal handed me contained instructions to report to the Base forthwith, thus abruptly terminating the afternoon's leisure.

To the accompaniment of a little furious thinking and some urgent self examination, I duly presented myself to the Naval Officer-in-Charge, to be informed by that gentleman that I was not "on the mat" as I feared, but that he "had a little job tor me". The British Army, he said, were retreating to the French coast, and, in company with all bases in Britain, we were to do our best to assist in the evacuation of troops and supplies from French ports.

All available craft were to be used and I was to be assigned to a small flotilla of tugs, which were to leave at 18.00 hours that evening and proceed to the coast of France, there to await instructions which would be provided when we contacted our destroyers.

A quick visit to my home, to check up on gas mask and helmet, and a speedy taxi eventually deposited me on a dock side where, with some misgivings, I gazed at the collection of marine craft on which we were to pin our hopes for the episode about to commence. And what a collection! Those four decrepit old harbour tugs may have gladdened the heart of any museum curator, but as instruments of succour to points on the French coast they seemed somewhat lacking. Many, many years old and of the usual coalfired—Scotch boiler — Reciprocating Engine type, it was extremely doubtful whether any of them had ventured more than 5 miles outside of any port in which they were normally employed.

The crews were a rugged conglomeration of individuals blessed with strong North Country accents and well equipped vocabularies. They were not at all keen on the job and one could hardly blame them. Their tempers had not been improved with the knowledge that they had been "taken over by the b----y Navy" until such time as evacuation operations were completed, and the sight of the gold-braided uniforms of the Commander R.N.R. and I, who were to be in charge of the little flotilla, did not wake rousing cheers from the assembled crews. Rough diamonds, those fellows, but coarse manners and natural resentment did not completely conceal their true worth, as subsequent events proved.

Sailing instructions from the Commander were brief and, in view of the fact that none of the four skippers possessed a chart or any instruments, almost unnecessary. He, with his own equipment and assisted by myself, would lead in one of the tugs, while the others were to play "follow my leader".

It was 21.30 hours before we managed to raise steam, and as we left the picturesque harbour, with tattered Red Ensigns bravely flapping in the cool evening breeze, our squadron of four harbour tugs steamed in "line ahead" with true Naval precision.

The evening wore on, the cliffs of England receding astern and a calm sea gave us time to settle down and take stock of the companions with whom we were to have our being for the next 4 days.

An evening meal was served, or rather thrown at us, by our ship's cook, a cantankerous individual who muttered strange oaths into his scraggy beard, and was understood to wish that the food would poison us! His wish was very nearly fulfilled. We had provisions enough for approximately four square meals all round, but as far as I was concerned anyone could have had my rations. Used to quick makeshift meals whilst "on the job" in harbour, the culinary prowess of tug cooks does not rise to great heights. Nevertheless the Commander R.N.R. did yeoman service with his knife and fork. He was a fine figure of a man, and one of the few monocled officers in the Navy. Aged about 50 he had seen an adventurous career and was game for anything. The "Mad Commander" I think they called him. He had a double-barrelled name which I can't give here and had stepped aboard direct from a spot of leave from whence an urgent telegram had recalled him.

With some little difficulty we gradually made ourselves at home with our strange hosts. Talk drifted, as usual, to ships, and on this common ground we gradually "broke the ice" with the taciturn skipper and his assistants (one could hardly call them mates !).

I had already inspected the engine room of our particular tug, so that when, later, I went into the depths to take a watch, I knew what to expect. We were extremely shorthanded and some of the crew had been transferred to the other three vessels, now ploughing along astern.

That first watch was a nightmare of hard work. Besides tending the 3 stage reciprocating engines it was also necessary for me to watch the decrepit old coal-fired Scotch boiler, and, what was more, to stoke it!

My experience with modern oil-fired plant in merchant and naval vessels had not bestowed on me the mighty muscles and great stamina common to personnel normally engaged in coalfiring operations, and two hands completely covered with huge blisters days later bore testimony to long hours of torture spent in wielding heavy rakes and massive coal-laden shovels into what must have been the highest furnace front afloat!

We sent the old tubs along at the cracking pace of approx. 6 knots, and on one memorable occasion, to the accompaniment of clouds of black smoke from grimy funnels, we must have almost reached 8 knots. We were in a hurry to get "over there" and the chugging old machinery groaned and creaked at the unaccustomed "forcing".

After long hours of this energetic form of watch keeping I was eventually relieved, to seek out what sleeping space was available in the poky little saloon for'd. Not one of us removed his clothes nor did we shave or wash during the 4 days that the operation lasted.

As a result of our frequently changing course, known only to the C.O. and necessary because of minefields, it was mid-morning before we approached the French coast, and an air of tension developed as each man realized that the real business of our mission was about to commence.

The Commander was busily engaged in trying to determine our exact position, and as I watched, he took a bearing on a distant object, making quick calculations in navigational mathematics.

Suddenly he stared at me and said "take off your hat!" Wondering, I did so, as with a laugh he explained "according to my calculations we're standing in Westminster Abbey, or thereabouts!"

The mystery was solved as we neared the object which he had taken to be a chart-marked rock. It was a barrage balloon, shot into the sea during some recent "incident".

At noon we anchored close inshore, there to await instructions. We could hear the distant rumbling of guns, and the sky throbbed to the roar of aircraft.

As the many planes approached us in various directions, the crews of our "flotilla" jumped to action stations. In the case of our tug, the only one possessing armament, this meant that four of us manned the two Lewis guns, situated on the bridge and up in "Monkey's Island". The remainder of the crew divided the two rifles between them and the Commander flourished his revolver. Thus we stood, ready for action!

After many false alarms in which we hastily "stood to" only to find that the passing aircraft were our own, we decided to ignore further engine noises until they personally affected us.

At 15.00 hours a solitary plane appeared and as we idly watched, it slowly circled and disappeared into the bright sun. Hardly had our skipper spat and muttered "one of ours", than we looked up to see twin jets of red flame spearing down at us from the attacking Junkers 87's guns!

We dived for our weapons, and did our best to thwart the evil designs of the youth who sat in his cockpit and sought to wreak destruction on 4 decrepit old harbour tugs at anchor.

One would have thought it a waste to aim bombs at such a target, but for the space of the next few minutes the water around our small craft was violently distributed by a pattern of bomb splashes as the German disgorged his entire unwelcome load.

He did not live to benefit from the practice he had gained. As he roared down in one of his gunspitting power dives, he came dead in the sights of the Lewis gun, whose tendency to jam at vital moments I had just mastered. One long burst and a full pan of .303 bullets sped into the black crossed Hun and as he looped away to fall into the sea, black smoke pouring from the crippled plane, I felt no pity for the unlucky crew.

Soon after this episode, we weighed anchor and steamed slowly in search of the British naval craft with whom we were to make our rendezvous. As dusk fell, a lean destroyer came alongside and without slackening speed, her captain called us through his "loud hailer" amplification equipment, ordering us to report with all despatch to one of the embarkation ports on the French coast.

Away she sped and with a re-adjustment to our course, we forged ahead, glad that our period of "stooging around" had ceased, and eager to be of service to the thousands of Tommies, now awaiting succour on the beaches and quays of the ports we were to make our destinations.

Of the next bitter 24 hours, all who have read the stories of Dunkirk, La Pallice, Brest, and other names not so familiar will know of the constant bombing, the harrowing scenes, in our case largely cloaked by a merciful darkness, and the general atmosphere of terror and heroism that epitomised the Great Retreat.

Detailed accounts of the evacuation scenes, in which small craft such as ours ferried exhausted troops from the crowded beaches to larger transports out in deep water, of the many gallant incidents and the too many grim stories are for another day and another writer.

Let it suffice here to pay a tribute to the crews of our tiny squadron, rough, honest harbour tug-men, who, like hundreds of others in yachts, launches and pleasure steamers from ports all round the coast of Britain, played their noble part in the saving of the vast quantity of men and material that would otherwise have fallen into German hands.

One of our jaunts took us as far as the great French naval port from which a substantial portion of the French Fleet steamed to the safety of English waters. It was stirring to see the grey giants steaming majestically out from their native harbour, with Tricolours flying, the engines of many submarines combining in a mighty roar of diesel power.

At the same port long lines of merchant ships, shepherded by watchful destroyers into two columns, arrived and departed, holds laden with precious war equipment. Further away, in this strictly marine tableau, the white painted, red crossed hospital ships went about their errand of mercy.

It was early on the fourth day when we finally left that scene of feverish effort, and as we steamed back into the friendly haze that was distant England, we blessed the luck that had brought us through the entire operation with no more damage than a badly shaken boiler and a few splinters.

We stepped ashore once more at Falmouth, dirty, unshaven and very tired, but proud that we had been privileged to take part in the operation that resulted in the saving of so many British lives.

ABOUT THE AUTHOR

THIS graphic article was written for me in 1940 by an old school friend, then Sub Lieut. Percy Mark Johns RNVR, a Falmothian. It has never previously been published.

Mr. Johns subsequently became the country's first television critic, writing for the Daily Express and then the Daily Sketch. He was chief public relations officer for the Pye Organisation then for the Association of British Industry and was a hugely successful campaign director of KEEP BRITAIN TIDY.

After rubbing shoulders with London's high society he turned his back on the bright lights and bought the Bowes Moor Hotel in upper Teeside. In 1984, five months after he had been reported missing, his body was found in a shallow moorland grave not far from the hotel.

After a lengthy trial two young hotel workers were found guilty of murdering him. One, aged 24, was jailed for life, and his accomplice, 19, was ordered to be detained at Her Majesty's pleasure

April 4, 1987

Diary records dramatic days in June 1940

I have been presented with a copy of a dramatic diary written by the late Evelyn Radford who with her talented sister Maisie was so well-known in the town. It covered nine hectic days in June 1940, and was first published in Cornish Review (No. 4) 23 years ago.

Miss Radford wrote: Tuesday, June 18: Electric Hire Co. says lights never returned from Princess Pavilion after opera (produced there by the Radford sisters). Ring up Pavilion, Police answer: Hall taken over for refugees. What kind? All kinds. Mrs. Green in charge of voluntary workers. Does she want help? Yes, all right, in case a rush comes and helpers all gone home. Rumour of 1200, no idea what or when.

Bordeaux refugees at Falmouth, Official war picture from the National Gallery

Wednesday, June 19: First arrivals, a boatload of survivors from the "*Lancastria*", torpedoed on her way home. Men, all sailors and soldiers, blackened and coated with oil, like the sea birds where oil fuel has been discharged. Rush for the canteen, the overflow lying out on the grass in the sun. "This is all right. I don't mind if I stay here for the duration." They drink very carefully, explaining, "We've too much oil inside."

Clamour for newspapers, we raid the nearest paper shops completely. "May I speak to someone in authority? I'm the purser," says one very gravely, and then laughing at himself, dressed in tattered navy trousers, no shirt and a kind of short duffle dressing gown. Missions to Seamen arrives with clothes to sort and distribute. The gardener's wife and some houses near offer baths in turns. All tired out and lie sleeping on the grass.

One little Belgian boy of 13, picked up and brought by the men, dressed in English soldier's uniform. Someone fits him out with shorts and shirt but he clings to the khaki tunic and forage cap. A Dutch theological college in some small vessel. Dispatched to workhouse to sleep. The big ship is coming, isn't coming, all day. At 9 p.m., a few hundred. Put on to distributing landing cards, instructing how to fill them in and explaining the routine: Landing cards, leave your luggage, medical examination, platform for passports, out by stage door, canteen. And the canteen hard at it, tea and bread and marge and bully beef galore, and how they eat. A glorious blaze of lights through the open doors! By 2 am most housed somewhere, some sleep on the spot by their baggage. Off to eat and bed about three.

Thursday, June 20: Meet last night's arrivals again: all extraordinarily cheery and good-tempered, but many of their stories pretty dreadful. Lloyds Bank manager from Brussels, with Belgian wife and pretty daughter, driving refugees until they became refugees themselves, five weeks from Brussels, from port to port, till Bordeaux, Boches behind and overhead, crawling a few kilometres an hour, getting out to lie in fields when planes close overhead. The girl escaped machine-guns by merest chance. Car abandoned at Bordeaux. All tell unforgettably the horror of the crowded roads.

A coal boat from Paimpol with a whole mercantile marine college, in charge of Pascal, a Breton artist—gay and charming as French boys can be. Apologies for being so black. Pascal says: 'N'importe, puisque j'ai mes gars." Some of them doing their final exam when word came of the Germans close to them. One of the boys heard by chance last boat leaving, and all rushed on board; some along the coast to join it on bicycles which arrive with them. Good to see them fall to and Pascal beaming round: "Quel accueil."

Will I go and talk to a girl trom Palestine, British subject but speaks little English. Find her reading music manuscript from her music case, she is Vera Shilonsky, a pianist and composer; the manuscript a new violin and piano sonata, very modern. She hoped to come to England, but not quite like this. Scribble one or two introductions hastily.

French Canadian nuns, with no English, rather helpless, but smilingly resigned, and shepherded by an Irish schoolgirl who shows them all what to do till they too are sent to the workhouse!

An Anglo-American young woman, who cannot make the officials believe that she left England exactly a week ago, flying over to meet her husband and daughter at her country house in the South of France, being put down at Tours in the moment of the German arrival and having to join the stream of refugees to Bordeaux, without ever getting near the husband and daughter.

Explanations complicated by the British white forms being headed non-British and the aliens. "Refugees from Holland or Belgium." History has moved too fast. Both cause great annoyance and mean incessant reassuring. Apart from personal posers like: "Please Madame, what must I say? I am British-born married a Belgian, divorced him, have no passport, and my children were born in France and are on one paper with me."

The 1200 can't be coming tonight. Buses are just coming up from the quay. A crowd suddenly. The advance-guard of the 1200, now 1300, subsequently 1600. The last boat out of Bordeaux with passenger room for 300!

August 18, 1990

Front line Falmouth - 1940

Last week I published the first part of a dramatic diary kept in June 1940 by the late Miss Evelyn Radford who with her sister Maisie did so much for the arts in Falmouth. They were working in the Princess Pavilion where refugees from Europe were arriving. Her cryptic comments capture the breathless mood of those hectic days when Falmouth was right in the front line and when no-one knew what the next few hours or days might bring. She continues her entries for:

Thursday, June 20: What a mix-up, civilians of all sorts, British subjects with remarkable English or none at all, French subjects speaking English perfectly, Malays with no known language (some just can, others can't sign their names); a sprinkling of Spanish republican survivors, livid at word "refugee"—sidelight on, their treatment; Polish Red Cross, Czech airmen, French and British all services, War Graves Commission, Imperial Airways, Standard Oil Co., Women's Auxiliary drivers, a young woman with several children and twin babies of five weeks ("We were lucky we knew at midnight that we should have to go, and had till morning to pack some things"). They pour in steadily, the luggage pile mounts to the ceiling, congestion awful. Customs, Immigration, and naval-military-cum "Yard" investigation, medical examination (perfunctory). At one time find myself interpreting in Polish which I don't know—(but find here and elsewhere that it works pretty well to speak Serbian until it clicks)—all in the hall. A splendid tempered crowd, all said and done; only about six complaints mostly about the little luggage they have been able to rescue one or two claiming priority for British subjects (if they realised which were the British subjects among them!), for young, for old, for "ex-servicemen."

The young woman I am directing is Virgina Cowles. She and the other American typically and untiringly determined to get the night train to town with their story. Another man: "Can I get up to the platform this way?" The amateur control: "Sorry, you must take your turn." 'Please get me through. I'm Edward Ward, of the B.B.C." Richard Capell sitting filling in his paper. Aid and abet him and his Telegraph colleagues to find a nearby telephone. All through the night an incessant stream. Moonlight streaming in and electric light out! Orpheus (three weeks before) haunts the strange scene like a lovely phantom. R.C. says, "to think how often I've wanted to come to Falmouth." One wouldn't be, and isn't, surprised at anything.

About 3 a.m. a man leans out of the queue: "You know the man in the hairnet is Baron Rothschild." Canteen never stops. At 5.30 the stream stops. Step out in the dawn over hundreds lying on the floor the verandah, grass and bandstand. Providentially, a perfect June night. Hundreds sent off already in the buses to work-house, cinemas, public halls, a few lucky to hotels, but the rest sleep soundly on the grass and everywhere. And as we are just driving off, two American girls stop the car just to say they feel they must thank somebody for their welcome.

Friday, June 21: Back after a grand breakfast, a lie-down without sleep and an early lunch. More boats arrived. The harbour crowded like the Golden Horn, or as M says, an old-fashioned picture of a naval battle. Tramps, trawlers, sailing boats, liners naval craft, and all the queer unnameable vessels that the war has brought forth, up the Roads, in the inner harbour and the fresh boatloads kept at the cinema while the rest of the big lot are cleared Queue at door a bit restive, and M. institutes a system of numbers. "Sit down and wait" in all languages. Luggage piles and Customs removed to verandah, and the plush tip-ups placed as for a performance.

A Russian-born interpreter with absolutely faultless English, Jean Bernard, the most mischievous Jew baby keeping the whole hall running, heaps of Poles. A crowd of them all want white tickets and think they have "diplomatic" passes. A perfect babel; pick out "juto" from the stream of words and call it out until they all get yellow tickets. Serbian fails sometimes; master the genuine Polish for the landing-ticket headings with the help of a diplomatic gentleman.

The sick and infirm, children of under 10 or so and their parents, up the "dress rehearsal" way to the stage A lot of care and explanation needed for this. "What is that man doing going up that way?" Call up to him: has he a young child? He holds up nine fingers and points to a sleeping heap of children on the floor in front. Children all have to go up as well as adults. Some of the nine lifted up promptly drop down asleep again on the stage. Closing time early this night, at 12.

Saturday, June 22: The worst day; rain and hours of waiting for the refugees on the quay. Odeon crowd frightened and restive. Short of facilities there, but helped out by Fire Brigade who supply boiling water from next door. Whitehall has got the wind up. Wait for reinforcement of officials. Immigration blames delay on Public Assistance. Public Assistance distracted and short in the temper. Poor refugees meanwhile wait unfed while we wait at the Pavilion, kick our heels, and institute a fresh series of numbers that we may be ready when officials do arrive. A lot through in smaller batches. Crews of three torpedoed boats, two British one Norwegian. A man from one of them borrows my pencil to make a list of the ship's stores lost, sucking the pencil and scratching his head over so many loaves, so many dozen tins of bully, a good steward.

All from small craft now, coal boats, cargo boats, trawlers. By the evening Organisation gets going. Sentries fixed bayonets, identity cards at the door and all. By the new system lavatories accessible only at the end of the long trail of formalities. Acting as escort there and back before the formalities becomes one of our jobs; past the fixed bayonets and the police in the garden. M. shepherds a family with small boys, a sudden skirmish, and half of them rush back to dive into the hall rummage in their bundles, extract a tin pot, and be re-escorted waving it in triumph past the police and the bayonets again.

Rest of Days: (Sunday-Wednesday): "Organisation" in full swing; sentries, armlets, police, threefold officials in each department. Fewer and fewer refugees. But nice small boat loads, a Belgian cargo boat, wildly over-passengered, a Norwegian trawler, heaps of Bretons (must have been the whole population of Le Portel, grannies in starched white caps, old men, fishermen in clogs, babies), many without their men, who are joining the fishing fleets. A greater reunion of the "Celtic "fisherfolk!

Another big lot rumoured, but finally go on to "another port." Fill in sheaves of landing cards for the Bretons. We have become Messages Department also, and the file grows fast of notes, "if so and so comes in, put them in touch with so and so. A lot have happily only got temporarily separated at landing and liaison wanted between the various groups.

A new uniform appears in the hall, a dapper French military. The young policeman to M. "Do you think he's all right—I have never seen a uniform like that, and he's muttering a lot to them. "

The Belgian liaison man running to know may he have an order on the canteen to take tea to the Mayor of Antwerp and the Speaker to the Belgian Parliament, in the Customs. Duly impressed, and take them a tray.

The over-passengered boat has acquired seven or eight Germans, rescued some say from another sunk, two or three in uniform, two women. Tea brought them while they wait for official enquiry. "Les Boches recevent du thé. Et les Anglais?..." says our Belgian quite gently. They look pretty happy.

As the pace slows, the officials multiply and become identifiable in their different departments. We have known the "Yard" for some time, almost too well got up, as in fiction! The amateurs fade out now, one by one, and boats will be few alas. But those first, those were the days, and the nights!

August 25th 1990

Falmouth defends itself for Second World War

Mr J.K. Petersen of Flushing tells me that in 1938, with war imminent, Falmouth took on a new significance. Its harbour and roadstead was the most westerly in the English Channel, capable of taking large, ocean-going ships and providing major repairs to damaged vessels.

The Admiralty started to take measures to protect the harbour and use the resources of the Fal to protect shipping. A boom defence was installed and gun emplacements began to appear around St Mawes and overlooking the lighthouse at St Anthony, as well as at Pendennis Castle. Anti-aircraft guns, searchlight batteries and barrage balloons arrived too.

Small boatyards began to play a major part in fitting out a host of small craft that were required in Falmouth harbour and elsewhere on the river. The Navy's presence became increasingly evident when war was declared in 1939.

Some older residents remember the issue of gas masks, identity cards and instructions for blacking out windows.

During the first few months of the war there was no bombing in the area and the local population concentrated on preparing for what was to come. Russell Smith remembers the Women's Voluntary Services using small boys, himself included at the age of eight, as runners for 6d a time. Later, villages such as Mylor Bridge had monthly gas mask drills which were held outside Miss Tresize's shop, now the Mylor Stores. The auxiliary fire services operated from a galvanised shed beside the oak tree in the playing fields where they had a big Dennis fire engine.

Other small communities around the Fal had similar organisations, responsible for passing on instructions to residents from higher authorities in Falmouth and Truro. Apart from air raid sirens, a flag was hoisted on St Anthony's Head to warn shipping and shore installations when a raid was imminent. It should be remembered that few private homes had telephones at this time.

Residents in Mylor Bridge had their own air raid alarm—a Great Dane belonging to Mr Rollason of the abattoir, opposite All Saints Church. The dog was reported to start barking a good 10 minutes before the planes arrived. This was not the only animal with remarkable powers. In 1943 the Cornish Echo carried an item by a visitor to a local farm who was told that they had a pig with "four ears", When questioned, the farmer replied; It's no freak, this is a commando pig with a pair of extra ears to listen for the approach of Jerry planes. When it hears one, it squeals the alarm!"

Not a lot was written about activities around the Fal during the first few months of the war. Normal sources, such as newspapers, did not publish such items because of censorship. Perhaps the most momentous event was the sinking of the aircraft carrier *Courageous*. Some of the survivors were landed in Falmouth. A number of merchant ships were torpedoed, but not sunk, and managed to limp in or were towed to Falmouth. The dockyard was kept busy repairing vessels.

As the war progressed, enemy aircraft started to bomb the area. The Cornish Echo of July 12 1940 had the headline 'Opened by Adolf Hitler'. Apparently a local Co-Op was about to be opened when the Germans paid a visit and one of their bombs blew in the front of the new shop. On the day of the official opening a sign at the premises read as the headline—'Opened by Adolf Hitler'.

David Spring of Mylor remembers a ship which was sunk off Penarrow Point. She was loaded with cotton and burned fiercely for several days.

When the Germans over-ran France the importance of Falmouth and its deep water harbour increased. The German bombers were now less than 100 miles across the Channel. A number of refugees escaped in small craft and were grateful to find refuge in Britain. A French minesweeper called 'La Suippe' elected to leave France and seek sanctuary in Falmouth. It was eventually taken up the Fal, but was later bombed by the Germans and sunk on Easter Monday 1941 on Tolverne Reach.

Len Richardson, who worked in the dockyard during the war, remembers a number of air raids with Germans bombing the dockyard. He recalls a bomb falling down the funnel of the *Tuscalusa* killing the master, Chief Engineer and several others. The *Durham* berthed at the Eastern wharf for repairs, had a parachute landmine dropped on her, but Len did not remember the extent of the damage or casualties.

This was a critical period of the war for the residents of Falmouth and the small communities surrounding it. Apart from the blackout and transport restrictions, rationing was becoming stricter and food supplies were much shorter than they had been. This affected the people in the big towns such as Truro and Falmouth more than those in the small communities where produce from the countryside was more readily available. Today, with new supermarkets opening in all the big towns, it is hard to relate to food rationing.

Some notes on food prices and other items are of interest. The

Ministry of Food announced that the maximum retail price of sugar would be reduced by 1d per pound. Revised prices would be: granulated sugar, 4^1/$_2$d per lb; cubed sugar, 4^1/$_2$d Another article in 1941 stated that: "The meat ration will be reduced next week from 1/2d to 1/-. The ration for a child to be reduced from 7d to 6d. The reduction was stated by the Ministry to be due to a decline in the numbers of home produced fat stock."

Basic commodities, even water, were in short supply, and to get a water supply to Mylor the residents had to use the justification that a prisoner-of-war camp had been set up at Mylor Cross Road, in the vicinity of Passage Hill. The Ministry of Health agreed to a loan of £1,150 (the difference in the cost between an uneconomic 3" and 6" water main). The Military authorities were also instrumental in helping to get the water main laid according to Mr Spear's records.

The area saw increasing numbers of foreign nationals displaced from Holland and France, as well as Norway. A Dutch training schooner was brought into Falmouth by the crew and was used as the headquarters for Dutch naval personnel, many of whom were in Enys Wood.

Mrs. Monica Cartwright was in the Wrens and stationed at Falmouth. She remembers a lot of the casualties and the subsequent landing of bodies in Falmouth. On some occasions she boarded damaged vessels as part of a team and had to lay out the bodies before they were placed in their coffins. She remembers all the different nationalities, including British, French, Dutch, New Zealand, Polish, Indian, Canadian, Australian and Norwegian, as well as Greeks and later Americans. She recalls the secret ops. room and Admiral's office at Membly Hall, which had a lawn on the left hand side where neat rows of barbed wire were camouflaged to look like cabbages.

Tony Warren of Falmouth is now a famous painter of ships and the sea. He was only aged nine at the time, but he remembers well many of the ships that appeared in the harbour. He has painted an important harbour scene with several vessels flying fish-tail balloons above them, as part of the defences. There were two sizes of barrage balloons—large for the land-based ones and small for the ships. Vessels engaged in coastal convoys were at one time fitted with kites to obstruct low-flying aircraft, but they were reported not to have been very successful. One balloon got loose and floated over Enys Woods. Eventually its wire caught in a tree and gypsies got it down and made shopping bags to sell out of the balloon fabric.

Large anti-aircraft batteries equipped with detection equipment and searchlights appeared on many of the hills around the Fal. Some were located at Tolverne, Feock, as well as Restronguet Farm and Trefusis

Farm. Mrs Trefusis recalls that there were two, sometimes three balloons in their field. They were fired on and came down when struck. She also recalls one being struck by lightning. They were made of silk all the local families supplemented their underclothing whenever this occurred!

Increasingly, the small Admiralty-owned dockyard at Mylor began to be used for a number of clandestine operations by the Free French and other units which landed agents on the coast of France, or undertook raids of one kind or another. George Corke of Mylor owned the small shed on the end of the jetty there; it was originally a sail store, but on occasions was used as a mortuary for bodies from vessels and boats that were sunk or burnt out. As war progressed its most important use was as a secret base for agents being shipped to France. Locals clearly remember four or five French fishing boats that used to come alongside and then disappear for periods of time before re-appearing. French sailors were frequently put ashore and the Free French fighters supplied with their documents prior to being sailed across the Channel. Most of this is confirmed by David Spring, Jimmy James and Derek Rowe. The old shack is now the new Mylor Yacht Club.

The attack on Russia by the Germans after their failure to invade Britain, brought the Russians into the war with profound effect. The Americans, under President Roosevelt, were becoming increasingly involved and, under an agreement between Churchill and Roosevelt, 50 old US destroyers were handed over in return for the use of some British bases in Bermuda and the West Indies. Old salts will remember that one of these old four stackers was named *HMS Campbeltown* and she was fitted out in the Fal prior to the attack on St Nazaire, in which she rammed the dockyard gates.

Mr J.K. Petersen who supplied the above information, gives thanks to the many people who contributed items from their personal memories and records. They include Joan Rea, Joan West, Jean Jefford, Colin Baptist, Jack Meek and the Kew Naval Record Office.

September 30th 1993

Dutch navy remembers those war years at Enys

'I was a stranger and ye took me in.' This sentence appears on a blue-tiled tablet on the wall of Falmouth Parish Church, commemorating the generous hospitality bestowed on the Netherlands sailors, soldiers and airmen during their stay in the area from 1940 to 1947 in the Second World War. The tablet was presented by the Protestant churches of the Netherlands.

The single sentence epitomises more than anything else the strength of the bond between Holland and Cornwall which resulted from links forged in the dramatic war years.

This week, from Mr Philip S. Niemeijer of Voorburg, I have received a magnificent book entitled 'Gedenkboek, Enys House 1940-1946' which is the definitive record of the occupation of Enys House, Penryn by the Royal Netherlands Naval College—an important phase in the history of the Royal Institute for the Navy.

The book, which includes a wealth of pictures, including prints old and new of Enys house and a study of Cmdr Robert Hichens, tells the

Prince Bernhard of the Netherlands at the entrance to the Municipal Buildings, being welcomed by the Mayor of Falmouth, Ald. Gill with Ald. W. Reep just behind.
Note: The sandbags for protection from bomb blast.

story of the Netherlands Navy during those hectic years and incorporates an English translation of the chapter 'Enys - the estate and the family'.

There is a foreword by the Admiral Prince Bernhard of the Netherlands, and chapters covering war and evacuation from the Netherlands with emphasis on the naval cadets who got away; Falmouth and the depot ship period; the trip to Canada taking Crown Princess Juliana and her children to safety, then a voyage by HNMS Sumatra to the Netherlands East Indies with the 1938 cadet entry on board; the establishment of the Royal Netherlands Naval College at Surabaya, the war against Japan and collapse of the Netherlands East Indies; the evacuation of cadets from there to Cornwall (Pill Farm, Lostwithiel then Enys); journeys of cadets who escaped from German-occupied Holland and overall the role played by Enys House.

The book, which is the end product of an immense amount of research, is partly based on official documents, personal logs, diaries and recollections.

A committee was set up in Holland to make all this possible, for while a number of reunions have been held at Enys, there appeared a remarkable dearth of official records about the period.

It was in June of last year at Mr Philip Fox's home in Mawnan Smith that I met Mr Niemeijer, who was visiting the area seeking information about the war years. He was introduced to Mr Bernard Breakell, author of 'Falmouth at War', who was also able to help. This near 200 page Gedenkboek is the result of that and other journeys made to the UK and in Holland and it is a remarkable testimony to the tireless efforts of all concerned who were attempting, after half a century, to record an epic chapter in the history of the Royal Netherlands Navy, which all who lived through the war will never forget.

The book explains that the 3,097 acres of Enys estate (now 1,200 acres) was the goal of the naval drafting proceedings on foot on July 20 1940. Carrick Roads was an excellent anchorage, Falmouth had ample port facilities and Enys stood in tranquil surrounds - ideal for training cadets.

The Enys family was proposing letting the house to the Royal Netherlands Navy for the training of cadets. Terms for the house were 1,000 guineas for a year; £950 per annum for two years and then £800 p.a. for five years.

In June 1940 the house and all else needed was requisitioned by the British Admiralty for the Netherlands Navy. However, in June 1944, an agreement was reached between the Admiralty and the Enys family, settling the amount of compensation to be paid backdated to the beginning.

In the summer of 1940 the house provided enough room for the continuation of the Royal Naval College, which had to be abandoned in the Netherlands as only a relatively small number of cadets had reached the UK who were not yet eligible for active service with the fleet. At first the Naval authorities had a short contract in mind because, at that time, a more permanent solution in the Netherlands East Indies seemed the obvious answer, as the greater part of the fleet was operational in those waters and new cadets would have to be recruited from there anyway. Developments were not slow in coming; at the beginning of August 1940 a substitute naval college was commissioned in Surabaya, while during the following year the Naval authorities seriously considered transferring the entire officers' training to Surabaya. Owing to the Japanese conquest of the Netherlands East Indies it did not come to this. On the contrary, after the lost battle of the Java Sea the Surabaya Naval College also had to be evacuated to England, so that by mid-1942 Enys House was in full operation again and even had to expand, the ARO-training (RNNR and RNNVR) being housed there as well. Enys House even continued to function as Royal Institute (Naval College) until one year after the liberation of the Netherlands, that is until April 1946 when the officers' training was transferred back again to Willemsoord on the Nieuwe Diep in Den Helder.

The name 'Enys' is an ancient Celtic name which means 'island', also 'clearing in the forest'. Possibly the name of the family is connected with the place where they lived.

The Enys family tree goes back to at least the year 1272 at the time of a certain Robert de Enys. In those days the estate was recognised by the Bishop of Exeter as a freehold estate, while Penryn received the Bishop's charter as a borough in 1236. Penryn belongs to the parish of St Gluvias and that is where the Enys family went to church and where they were buried. In the parish church there is a memorial stone with the family coat of arms clearly and handsomely carved in relief. The estate also plays a part in the Cornish mediaeval drama 'Origo Mundi'.

The old house, a Tudor house from approximately the end of the 16th century, burnt down in 1826, after which the present Enys House was built in 1830 at a cost of about £6,700. To ensure that, should there ever be another fire, there would not be an insufficient supply of water, a few reservoirs were constructed in the vicinity in which, or so the story goes, the cadets occasionally went swimming. The reservoirs are still there but in the meantime they have become overgrown with weeds, bushes and shrubs.

After 40 years unoccupied, both house and gardens have lapsed into a somewhat neglected state.

On December 31 1991 Elizabeth Enys died, the last person who bore the name of the Enys family. Without doubt many of those who had their training at Enys House will remember her.

When the Royal Netherlands Navy left Enys in 1946 and returned to the Netherlands, they presented the mayors of Falmouth and Penryn with a plaque to be attached to their chains of office. It is a small brass shield, approximately 5 x 3cms, displaying a foul anchor and crown. Above the letters KM on the back, the following text was engraved:

'Presented to the citizens of Falmouth (Penryn) by the Royal Netherlands Navy, 1940-1946'.

May 23, 1992

RAF Barrage Ballon site on the Beacon. US Quonset hut in background

Good friends from Holland

THE story, a couple of weeks ago, about the production in Holland of a book to commemorate the sojourn of the Royal Netherlands Navy at Enys from 1940-46, revived a host of memories for former Falmouth harbour tug skipper Mr Gordon Martin, now resident in Penryn. With remarkable clarity Mr Martin recalled the names of the following Dutch naval vessels: *Jacob van Hemskirt*, cruiser minelayer (big); *Jan van Gelder*, a large cruiser; *Vanhoedenof*, coaster carrying naval supplies; *Yusa basi Haki*, minelayer (possibly Turkish), captured by the Dutch; *Mirage*, a large shallow draft waterboat; *Swartsee* and *Roedzee*, deep sea rescue tugs, both under naval flags *Hydrograf*, used for Dutch cadet training - she moored off Greenbank Quay; *Actop*, a steam vessel which worked in conjunction with one of our own large motor yachts, the *Arlette*. They were at the entrance to the harbour, by a boom, off St Anthony Head. *Hydrograph* and *Actop* were well-known vessels, having served longer in the port than any other Dutch craft. Another ship recalled was the large cargo passenger liner *Batavia*, which was later sunk.

Mr Martin told me that during the Enys years his father had been appointed by the Dutch Admiral, in conjunction with Admiral Thesiger, to catch fish for the Dutch navy personnel. There had been trouble with a local buyer who would not supply petrol and paraffin coupons because Mr Martin senior sold his own fish.

In 1943 Mr Martin senior was machine-gunned by two ME 109s when his boat was fishing in the Manacles/Kennack Bay area. His young mate Walter Hedgecombe ('Hedgie') brought him ashore to the port hospital.

On Greenbank Quay all the locals became firm friends with the crews of the *Hydrograph* and *Actop* and in the mackerel season 'Cookee a Low' from the latter vessel would bring ashore for Mr Martin's parents some of the mackerel, beautifully smoked. 'The way they did them was delicious,' said Mr Martin. A number of the Dutchmen married local girls. One was Henk van der Hoeven who married Maud Coote and made his home in Falmouth. 'He was a very good friend of mine who sadly died last year,' said Mr Martin.

He explained that all vessels came under the RNN control, including the tugs. Crews including Mr Martin's father and mate (Hedgie) got concessional extras as a result of a covenant made by Queen

Wilhelmina. These included extra food rations, toothpaste, soap etc. All Dutch ships, whether naval or commercial, obtained these extras.

'Dutch ships,' added Mr Martin, 'as most seamen know, were beautifully kept and it was a rule that any member of a crew who elected to work out of duty hours and who went to the captain or officer in charge and offered to do any maintenance work were paid extra. This was known as "interest work" and the privilege was even extended to our own DEMS gunners when sailing in a Dutch vessel.'

While speaking mainly about Dutch ships, Mr Martin pointed out that after Dunkirk there was a mass of every type of Continental vessel in the harbour and bay. There were literally hundreds of every type and the examination service proved a nightmare. Mr Martin referred to work done by a local man, Mr Mark Johns - a captain in the Army at the time - who carried out examinations in the Odeon cinema.

Mr Martin said one of the problems was to keep the many ships supplied with drinking water. The water ships did their best. On the King's Wharf at the docks were hundreds of empty jerrycans. Whenever the tug went out hundreds of these were filled with water and passed to the vessels in the bay.

He is convinced of Divine providence and says that as the Red Sea opened to allow the Israelites to escape, so during the whole 1940 period the weather remained perfect.

In earlier years Mr Martin served as coxswain in the motor launch *Undine* and he remembered the vessel leading in the former *USS Buchanan* (renamed *HMS Campbeltown*) to number 5 buoy. She was the famous ship used in the raid on St Nazaire. They also ferried members of the number 5 Commando to and from *Campbeltown* and he got to know many of them well. Ironically, later in the war, when he was skipper of the tug, *St Levan*, he took another old ex-American four stacker (four-funnelled) destroyer to the same buoy. She was being used in a film about the St Nazaire raid entitled 'Gift Horse' and starring Trevor Howard. Much was shot in and around Falmouth. Referring back to the incident concerning his father's ship being machine gunned, Mr Martin said that at the time he was mate in the steam tug *Fairnilee* on station off the Western Wharf. A good friend on board the Dutch examination vessel *Actop*, on station off St Anthony, signalled to him the bad news that his father had been seriously wounded.

Mr Martin said: 'For this I will always be grateful to RM Sgt James Lawson who was the yeoman on station. Sadly he is now dead.

'He came on the tugs as an able seaman after his demobilisation and also served in the Falmouth lifeboat crew for a time. His widow lives in Oakfield Road, Falmouth.'

June 20, 1992

Dutch sisters' enquiry

HALF a century since the last world war, memories of those momentous years in Falmouth continue to surface.

Two Dutch sisters who were staying in Par recently paid a surprise visit to the Maenheere Hotel at Grove Place, Falmouth.

There they said their father- Hendrek Heida, of Ragenborg, Heerenveen, Holland had obtained his Master's ticket at a Dutch navigation school held in the hotel during the war. They wanted to see where their father had qualified and were seeking further news of the school and a chance to meet any people who were there.

The hotel's present proprietors, Mr and Mrs Bernard Smales, did not own the hotel at the time.

They would be pleased to receive any information from anyone who has memories of this school, which they will forward to the family in Holland.

September 26, 1992

Castle guns fired once in anger

Coastal defence guns at Pendennis Point only fired once in anger during the 1939-45 war. That was when it was believed there were several German 'E' boats lurking near the Manacles waiting to pounce on a convoy. The results of the action were never known.

There are now only three or four men still alive who served at Pendennis and St Anthony during the war.

One of them, 75-year-old Mr Victor Simms, now of Penryn, was a sergeant in the Royal Artillery. He told me he had joined an anti-aircraft regiment with the Territorial Army before the war, equipped with three-inch guns. When war was declared new guns were installed at Pendennis and St Anthony.

In preparation for coastal defence work three groups of men were sent for training: 1, to Drake's Island; 2, Fort Bovisand (Mr Simms went there); and 3, Stadden Heights, behind Fort Bovisand.

In about six weeks time two six-inch high angle modern coastal defence guns were sited at Pendennis and the original weapons from there, which dated back to the 1914-18 war, were moved to St Anthony. Supervised by a regular soldier, an RSM from Woolwich, the guns were calibrated across the bay.

There was a searchlight battery under Pendennis and another under St Mawes Castle. A local man named Stangroom was with the lights and Harry Snell RE was at the castle.

Shortly after that Mr Simms was promoted to sergeant and he was responsible for an intake of new recruits. These were billeted in a hotel on the sea front which was bombed. RSM Charlton was in charge of this intake.

The guns were manned by members of the 201 Battery RA, commanded by Major Stephens of Ponsanooth and with him were Lt A Banfield and Lt D Horder.

Mr Simms said he moved several times between Pendennis and St Anthony. The guns at Pendennis, known as the Half Moon Battery, were in emplacements below the castle and were reached through a tunnel from the Castle.

Both Mr Simms and Mr Horder were on the vantage point of Pendennis when Falmouth and the docks were bombed. One bomb also fell on the barracks block at the Castle. They described the amazing sight of the bay filled with ships at the time of Dunkirk (and never bombed!) and of seeing hundreds of returning troops sitting on the grass by the castle waiting to be entrained to other parts of the country. All had to be screened because of the danger of fifth columnists infiltrating. Many of the bigger ships were not allowed through the booms into the inner harbour and troops had to be brought ashore from them.

Mr Simms was eventually posted to a course in Plymouth. This was during the blitz and much time was spent retrieving bodies from bombed houses. After that he was posted to the Field Artillery, eventually ending up in Germany from where he was demobilised. When he briefly returned to Pendennis it was to find only one man—Sgt Stan Jenkin— remained from his former colleagues. All had been posted overseas.

Later, twin six-pounders were sited by Crab Quay and at St Mawes with the late Sgt Major Harry Westcott in charge. Another local man remembered was pay clerk Stuart Wells of Falmouth who was with the searchlight unit.

Mr Horder ended up in the Channel Islands helping to accept the surrender of the German troops there.

November 4, 1993

Memories of Dad's Army

On February 13 1939 young Frank Colenso of 12, Berkeley Hill, Falmouth joined the staff of the "Falmouth Packet" as a trainee reporter. Within a few months he was the sole staff member with the then editor, Mr. J. E. Prior. All the others had gone to war. From 1940 until 1942, when he was conscripted and joined the Royal Air Force, Frank became a member of the LDV, later to become the Home Guard.

His war service took him to Burma and Japan. After demobilisation he worked in the Royal Aircraft Establishment at Farnborough where he now lives.

Home Guard parade on The Moor

During those memorable years from 1940 to 42 he kept a very personal day-by-day diary. Recently he looked out these diaries and has now extracted many of the relevant entries.

They are unique and provide a remarkable record of the times.

A full set has been given to Mr. Peter Gilson at the Royal Cornwall Polytechnic Society for his historical records of Falmouth. Unfortunately space does not permit complete reproduction, but I have picked out a number of entries, which I am sure will stir memories of those still surviving who were members of Dad's Army half a century ago.

With the diary extracts Mr. Colenso has included a series of comprehensive explanatory notes some of which I hope to publish next week.

Here are some of the diary entries: 1.1.40 Air raid warnings sounded 9.30am. Tests to be repeated first Monday each month. 1.6.40 Dunkirk soldiers land. Mum nursing them at hospital (Red Cross). 5.7.40 First air raid on Falmouth. 6.7.40 Afternoon air raids. Evening - joined LDV cycling patrol, age nearly 16. 7.7.40 Air raid. Lister street and Windsor Quarry hit. Geoffrey Maynard's house hit. 10.7.40 Papered workshop windows (air raid precaution) Went to cemetery. Funeral of Sunday's air raid victims. 11.7.40 My 16th birthday. Two air raids in morning. 13.7.40 First patrol with Bullen and me, Mawnan and Constantine. 19.7.40 Evening patrol with Lewis (vicar of Penwerris) and Gibbons to Maenporth. 25.7.40 Found small piece of shrapnel at parish church. 31.7.40. 9 am patrol with Lewis around Port Navas. 20.8.40 HG patrol. Left but were all sent home because of air raids. Bombs on docks. 22.8.40 No air raid warnings!! 3.9.40 War for one year now. 9.9.40 Patrol Crag Maenporth (manoeuvres). 19.9.40 Fire Harris' coal yard. 20.9.40 Foot drill All Saints Hall (Cyclist Patrol with 4 others). 24.9.40 to be issued with with arms on 27th 27.9.40 Drill Hall. rifle drill at Belmont in dark - OK 29.9.40 Cycle patrol (6 of us) looking for lights (1½ hrs) 30.9.40 Continued making drill rifle 9.10.40 Joined Home Guard-in section 2. Four air raids and it's raining! 14.10.40 .22 rifle range (15 rounds) one bull 15.10.40 First guard duty at Swanpool, with Nick and Joe Beckett. On for one hour.20.10.40 Sunday Shooting .303 at Calamansack had four bulls out of five (19 out of 20) 21.10.40 Guard duty Swanpool. Issued with respirator. 13.11.40 Parade and gas test. 19.11.40 Drill and bayonet practice. Issued with great coat, bayonet and frog. 24.11.40 route march through town, sea front and cemetery. 26.11.40 Lecture on Morse Code which I have to learn in two weeks. 28.11.40 got paid 3/- and also got bandolier. 8.12.40 Guard duty Swanpool. New guard room with BUGS. Dispute and some went home. NO SLEEP THERE! 17.12.40 Lecture by Col Weymess - OK (Secret). 20.12.40 Guard for 2 hrs 40 mins. I am now officially in Home Guard and am 16 yrs 5 months and 9 days old. 29.12.40 Sunday exercise. Pill box in valley flooded out. Good defence. 31.12.40 Parade evening. 25 rounds ammo issued. I now have 45 (5 short of the 50) 1.1.41 Ice on Swanpool. Guard night. Played football. 4 hours sleep. 5.1.41 Field day exercise till 4. I was stretcher case. 12.1.41 Sunday. B... awful exercise. 21.1.41 Five rounds issued. Have my 50 now. 25.1.41 Guard duty. darkened leather anklets and belt. Joe told us off (Joe Beckett). 29.1.41 Signallers' class at Coast Lines instead of DCLI drill hall. First-class on flags. 31.1.41 Last guard at Swanpool cafe. Going to Trescobeas next. Fish and chips and singing. 18.2.41 Guard duty Nick, Jeff and Bolo (Eddy) in NAAFI five hours' sleep, Trescobeas, Snow and hail , rejected offer to join HG Intelligence Corps 9.3.41 six of us carried sandbags on railway line all morning. Got tin hat but no strap 25.3.41 Parade. Plans for parachutists. 7.4.41 Guard duty and patrol

Penryn Home Guard

in air raid looking for lights . 11.20pm to 1.20am. 9.4.41 . Saw bomb crater with Bill Ward near Hydro hotel and railway line big un! 13.4.41 Nick, Bolo, Kelway, Cortis and Jeff in afternoon to Penryn reservoirs etc. Guard duty, Dark no patrol.20.4.41 Exercise Enys Woods, Roskrow. Dinner in wood with home brew OK. Slept all evening 21.4.41 Platoon route march through Budock. 30.4.41 Parade and duty with shoes on Rifle drill and marching in rain NAAFI and chips. 7.5.41 All night air raid. 10.5.41 Shoot at Idless range - went by Army lorry. 12.5.41 Bombs on Penryn and on Wesley and on Pearce, Wayside and Wellington and Wodehouse terraces. 18.5.41 Idless range. got 9 bulls out of 10 rounds five with gas mask on. Best shot there and won the kitty 23.5.41 With Nick to Stithians to see results of bombs. Got 6 pieces of shrapnel. 25.5.41 Church parade parish church. Raining. Guard duty night at Ponsharden. Air raid. Fired Lewis gun but it jammed and cocking handle flew out. Only fired single shots at aircraft, cocking each time with jack knife. Kelly and Bolo fired one each in water on the Falmouth lifeboat and other boats

1.6.41 Sunday exercise at Flushing. Rotten. Got bombed with 'potato mashers' Home at 3 pm then slept $19^{1}/_{2}$ hrs 18.6.41 Exercise near Budock. Guard duty Ponsharden. In boat wlth 5 others. Nearly shot in head by RAF barrage balloon men because we did not stop boat when challenged. 12.7.41 Night air raid Ponsharden Guard. Fired Lewis at enemy a/c. Noisy. Now have 8 spare rounds (pinched five from Lewis). 18.7.41 Saw Miss Hick at Marlborough road after her house was bombed. 30.7.41 Guard (missed another 1/6d not being able to parade first). 11.8.41 Guard. Marched via Budock (pub and drink) to Maenporth (Crag). OK. Picked 5s worth of apples in orchard. Home late in morning. 10.9.41 Guard duty with Nick who joins RAF next Wednesday. Dog watch. Pay night (17s). 22.9.41 Guard at Pendennis Castle. Lost 2s and someone changed my bayonet for a rusty one. 10.10.41 Guard early start at Castle (there for good) Bolo lit fire. Getting colder now. Long alert. 28.10.41 Guard at castle (six of us) Slept in one room (cat sh . . in other). 21.11.41 Parade. .22 shooting. I won a packet (20) of Craven A - sold to Kelly for 1/6d. got water bottles now. 10.12.41 Parade then guard duty. Misty rain. Pop Fittus is going into RAF. 15.12.41 guard duty. Issued with gas cape. rolled up on shoulders. Last guard with Kelly and Bolo at O.P. on cliff at Pennance. 21.12.41. Shoot at Calamansack. .303. Won 2/10d sweepstake for best shot. 3.1.42 Night exercise from 5.30pm to 2pm next day. Took supper to pillbox on railway (Trescobeas) and patrolled all night. Pinched half hour's sleep under railway arch. Fried sausages in am. 12.2.42 got home 9.5pm. No alert for a change—broke Thursday night record! 13.2.42 Parade and lecture in Drill hall about HG in Cornwall. Pay night (17/6 highest yet) Bought HG flashes for sleeves of tunic. Handed in my Springfield rifle, bayonet, ammo. frog, scabbard, oil bottle and pull-through in exchange for .303 rifle (Canadian Ross dated 1918,) with short bayonet, ammo. etc. Don't like it much yet. May fire it Sunday week. Five spare rounds from Pop Fittus and seven clips. It has an aperture sight and a quick straight bolt action. 25.2.42 Drill and parade. Cold and frosty. Wrist watch going OK (the one I got from Bolo Eddy for a cigarette lighter which had cost me 10d). 14.3.42 Sat night exercise (9pm to 1.30am) Nansidwell Hotel and Bream Cove. Dark and muddy but all OK. 21.3.42 Sharpened bayonet and knife in workshop. Guard after parade when we cleaned grenades (Mills 36) and primed them. took two grenades to OP (Pennance) Field telephone there. Back to clubhouse (guardroom). 27.3.42 on to London for weekend. Met Nick there. Went to Windmill saw Vic Oliver. 11.4.42 Exercise. Creeping around the Crag at Maenporth till 2am. Not bad. 17.4.42 Cycled to Maenporth and walked to Pennance OP. Found torch. Took it to replace the one shot up by Robbie Gill's Browning automatic accidentally firing one round through a torch plus two blankets one mattress, bunk door post and floor (it took some stopping!). 9.5.42 Parade at Coast Lines for exercise at Flushing. Landed there from rowing boats and climbed cliffs, hedges and fields to get on roads. After marching for hours reembarked for Greenbank. 17.5.42 Anniversary parade in rain. Marched to Ashfield, main street and sea front. Raining all the time. 20.5.42 Exercise near Mawnan against officers. 31.5.42 Company HQ exercise at Hayle. Went to Hell's Mouth in lorries then advanced to sand dunes. Dinner at Hayle in hot sun. Home 6pm Sunburned now. 1.6.42 Field exercise at Five Fields. Guard duty. Two raid warnings. Making cigarette lighter from .300 cartridge case and bullet. Sold it later for 8s. 13.6.42 Going to Weston Super Mare tomorrow to see about aircraft factory job. Missed parade and no guard duty (no pay night!). 26.6.42 Notified I have got job at Weston. 2.7.42 Drill Recreation Ground then guard duty, Mum made egg and bacon pasty - very filling. Kelly to join R. Navy. 5.7.42 Up at 8.15 (Sunday) for shooting at Calamansack. Home 2.45, ten minutes for dinner then back again - 17 out of 20 at 300 yds two at 400 yds (awful) and nil at 300 yds (after running 100 yds wearing gas mask). 12.7.42 Exercise all morning then went to Rosemullion (our mortar post with new (conscript) HG recruits. 18.7.42 Exercise at 9.30pm. In park till 11.30pm then out to degaussing station by lorry. Bream Cove Nansidwell Mawnan Bareppa Budock Crill and Golden Bank on FOOT then lorry took us home 2.20am. 24.7.42 Showed printing office staff my .22 pistol in the making. Think its OK. Working on it one month now. Cpl (Lukie) Ronald Gay our gaffer in HG is joining RN Tuesday. Dougy Marts taking his place. 27.7.42 No more news about my job yet. 20.8.42 Left work 7.35pm HG duty after 8 parade (gas lecture) Pennance first guard with recruit. Had 3 hours sleep there (a record). 23.8.42 Exercise. Went to College Woods Penryn with Doug Martin and others. Did NOT get shot! 12.9.42 Not going to Weston now as government took over factory. Not sorry. 10.10.42 Shooting at Rosemullion Head with Donald Searle and 10 other company snipers led by Lieut. Hosking and Sgt. Ken Williams. 25 rounds each firing at about 100 and 250 yards at tins in water and on rocks. Knocked down 8 or 9—good shots from cliff edge. Best shooting I've been to. Hoping to do this every Saturday afternoon. 24.10.42 Evening exercise between Pennance and Maenporth. Ambushed and worried the other platoon. Got 'shot' walked into Maenporth. Home at 1am (walked home) Not bad. Blacked out face with burnt charcoal and wore my 'commando' woolly hat. 30.10.42 Johnny Rendle 'Cornish Echo' wrote his Scribbler column about me this week—very funny. 5.11.42 By train to Plymouth for RAF medical and interview at Mannamead. Medical A1 - have to go to Oxford in week or so. 13.11.42 Got pass for Oxford (Plymouth first) for aircraft hand u/t for air crew—that's me! Evening parade and map reading. 20.11.42 Train to Plymouth. Arrived 11am recruiting depot. Met 2 other chaps and went to Oxford after 2/- dinner. Got there 8.30 reported to RTO. Had supper and slept at YMCA after spending half hour looking for it. Up at 6.45, washed and breakfast. 8.10. Got to laboratories 8.40 had medical (one ear and one eye below standard) had intelligence maths and morse code tests. Told them I'd like to be flight mechanic now. Signed on, sworn in —OK. Reporting to Warrington next Monday. Stopped Plymouth. Toc H. slept on chair. Home 8am glad I got flight mech job. 24.11.42 Handed in all HG kit. Said goodbye to colleagues. 27.11.42 Finished work at 'Falmouth Packet.'

June 9, 1990

On guard in 1940 against Hitler's hordes

Last week I published extracts from the wartime diary of Falmothian Frank Colenso, who in 1940 before he was 16, joined the LDV and later the Home Guard.

With the diary he sent notes which paint an interesting picture of life in those heady days. Here are some extracts.

He writes: My particular pal in Platoon (No 2) was Ken Kelway "Kelly" who was a milkman with the Co-op on a horse-drawn round. His H.G. boots suffered more wear than most, trudging round Falmouth, needing frequent repairs, for which he was always reprimanded.

Roy Jackett and Bill Ward, "Cornish Echo" reporters in Falmouth were both killed in the war —Roy, I think, only lasted six months in the Army. Bill, whose father managed the butchers, or grocery, a few doors from old Coplins shop in Killigrew Street, was air gunner in RAF Bomber Command, and was killed in (perhaps) 18 months. Charlie T. Nicholas, a mutual friend, who also went into the RAF, then lost an arm later on, died a few years after the war. Eddy, "Bolo", worked at Marks & Spencer. Their top price was 5s. against Woolworths 6d., and I remember their watches at 4s. 11d. for instance (25p). Joe Beckett had been one of the four masters at our C. of E. Boys School (by All Saints Church) and was our Sgt. for a while, and we didn't perhaps show our old respect to him now that we had left school!

Stafford F. Hough was Company Commander. The name Osborne in the diary, I think, was the photographer brother of E. T. Osborne, our headmaster, but I can't be certain. Many of the diary entries only use forenames, nicknames, or shortened surnames which doesn't help in recalling their full names, at this stage. The Vicar of Penwerris (Lewis) was in charge of the LDV Cycling Patrol, which took us out at night round the villages and lanes of the areas round Falmouth. Our only armament was his little automatic pistol with its clip of only seven rounds, and he was very upset when old Charlie Pullen (who, I think, lived bottom of Berkeley Hill (by B. Vale) and had a fish-selling business with a hand-barrow round the town) returned the gun with one round missing. Vicar's words to him were not quite the ones used by men of the cloth! Charlie was an old soldier with endless stories for our young ears.

Other names: Lewis, Jeff, Osberg, Sgt. Maj. Sandy, Col. Wemyss,

Tubby, Ken, Cort (Clifford Cortis) who was in P.O. Later, he was gunner in motor-gun boat (a good marksman) and later was harbour master, etc. at St. Michael's Mount for many years, until loss of one eye made him leave and retire. Col Wemyss, Mr. Rogers, Trevarthen, "Pop" Fittus (Falmouth Packet, Printing).

Sgt. Cliff Roberts (who lived next door to me in the last house in Berkeley Hill) was Dock's deep sea diver. After H.G. exercise ended at top of hill leading to Ferry Boat Inn at Helford, just before closing time, we all ran downhill, sparks flying off our studded boots, for a drink.

It was my first visit to a public house. Cliff asked what I would drink. I was very thirsty, and naturally I asked for a glass of water, please! What I didn't quite understand was everyone's amazement at my request, but the barman complied. Cliff had a cheaper round, and I enjoyed my first pub drink from a big pint glass. Later, though, being introduced to beer, I enjoyed the pub visits on our exercises and I recall also that we were given the right to use the Services NAAFI canteen, where the strangle-hold of the local brewery mafiosi was broken by the sevenpence-a-pint Naafi beer. It was overlooking the Moor car park, over the Bus Station, I believe, though there was another services canteen near to the Docks we sometimes used.

L/Cpl. Collins, Richard, "Happy" Hunt, Gibbons, Capt. Stewart Brown, Robbie Gill (had the Browning Automatic rifle). I was glad I didn't have it, because of its extra weight and extra ammunition! Sgt. Marsden, Lt. Richard Davy Brown, Bullen Cpl. (Lukie), Ronald Gay (our gaffer!), Harold Wilkes, Charlie Pullen, Doug Martin (Marts), Keen ("Happy" or "Brother"), L/Cpl. Tyler, Charlie Jones, Donald Dearle, Lt. Hosking (who led our guerilla platoon which I was in, as sniper, one of about a dozen), Sgt. Ken Williams, Geoffrey Maynard, Ken "Bolo" Eddy (worked in Marks & Spencer) I believe had a Browning Automatic rifle, as he was a big lad.

We enjoyed the shooting on the rifle ranges— at Truro and Calamansack—once our developing sixteen-year old shoulders got toughened to the powerful recoil of our .303 and .300 cartridges.

We were always on the scrounge for some extra rounds of "ammo", which we jealously hoarded, and our rifles were carefully maintained, always cleaning barrels through after firing, with plenty of boiling water. It was a laugh getting issued with everything—it went on for months, getting odd pieces of equipment now and again.

Doing night guards in winter at the Castle Drive, with an army blanket for warmth—we were like the Spanish Civil War guerilas. As an aside, I am reminded of the Basque Spanish children evacuated from Bilbao (1937 or 1938 I believe) from that war zone.

As I remember, about 20 in our party were found foster families in

Falmouth by the Falmouth Labour Party, of which my father William Colenso was treasurer, some families taking two to keep brothers or sisters together.

We kept in touch for many years after. My mother, Florrie Colenso, did voluntary Red Cross nursing, and so was on duty at Falmouth Hospital when the soldiers were brought there from Dunkirk. Later she had soldiers of the 5th Commando billeted on her and also American soldiers, with whom she had a special affinity, having spent her own childhood in Montana, when her father, a Cornish mine carpenter, brought up a family until returning early this century.

Sadly, he died a year later, and so my granny Williams raised the family single-handed on a small-holding just opposite the old tin streaming works on the Redruth-Portreath Road.

Grandfather Colenso drove the coach-and-four between Falmouth and Penzance regularly and Dad's sister Nellie (Barnicoat, when she married) used to have to go to the field, catch the horses and ride them to the stables bare-back. I could never imagine her doing it! My father was a boilermaker at the Docks.

In his early apprenticeship he worked on a number of the old mine beam-engine boilers in Cornwall. He died in 1948. I still have postcards he sent from Southampton, where he worked in the *Queen Mary*, 1937 approximately, when the smoky funnels were modified, over a period of weeks, which gave welcome work after such a lot of laying-off and dole-time common to the twenties and thirties. He was a fire-watcher in the town during the war.

In spite of food rationing, mother never failed to provide me with an egg-and-bacon pasty on guard-nights, and considering this was each sixth night, it was there without fail—a sustaining supper if ever there was one!

As local boys, familiar with Falmouth and surrounding villages and lanes, we were ideal as the cycling patrols, in the early days, just silently going out and about in darkness looking for the unusual.

We dug trench systems, sand-bagged parapets, made mortar positions (especially permanent fixed spigots for our Blacker Bombard mortar) where we knew all the ranges of the immediate ground, and the weapon could be quickly mounted and loaded.

Round the coast paths we patrolled and we had at times glow worms guiding part of our night walks from the Crag Hotel at Maenporth. When we got soaked with rain, or damp with dew, it was accepted as normal and we were not often cold. When I joined the RAF (late in '42) I was introduced to frosts, snow and ice for the first time.

Brother Jack, three years older, started at Murt's electrical shop on the Moor, as an electrician, following his time at the Grammar School.

He was a keen sportsman —wrestling, water polo, rugby, etc. and played for Falmouth and also for Cornwall, as hooker.

He then worked at the Falmouth Docks as marine electrician and was not allowed to join the services as the job was "reserved".

He was in the A.F.S. there and got involved with tanker fires etc. during that period until he joined the RAF in 1943, trained as pilot in South Africa on Spitfires, Tempests and Typhoons in the Middle East. He was sorry not to take part in the war in Europe, which was over when he was fully trained, and I found an entry in my Burma diary of '45 where he had written he hoped to join me out there soon. In 1955 he moved to South Africa where he has been working and living and has settled in the Transvaal.

For several years he flew there in his own Cessna 150 aircraft, and his work mostly takes him to South African Air Force bases, now.

Our family name was given to a town in Natal, on the Tugela river, which runs towards Durban, by our ancestor (great, great, etc.,etc. grandfather Bishop John Colenso) who was Bishop of Natal in the mid-1800s.

June 16, 1990

Members of the Home Guard take part in the exercise "Stand Easy"

German View of Falmouth

For the second time in my life an unusual memento of the Second World War has come into my possession. It is a German aerial picture of Falmouth oil tanks and docks.

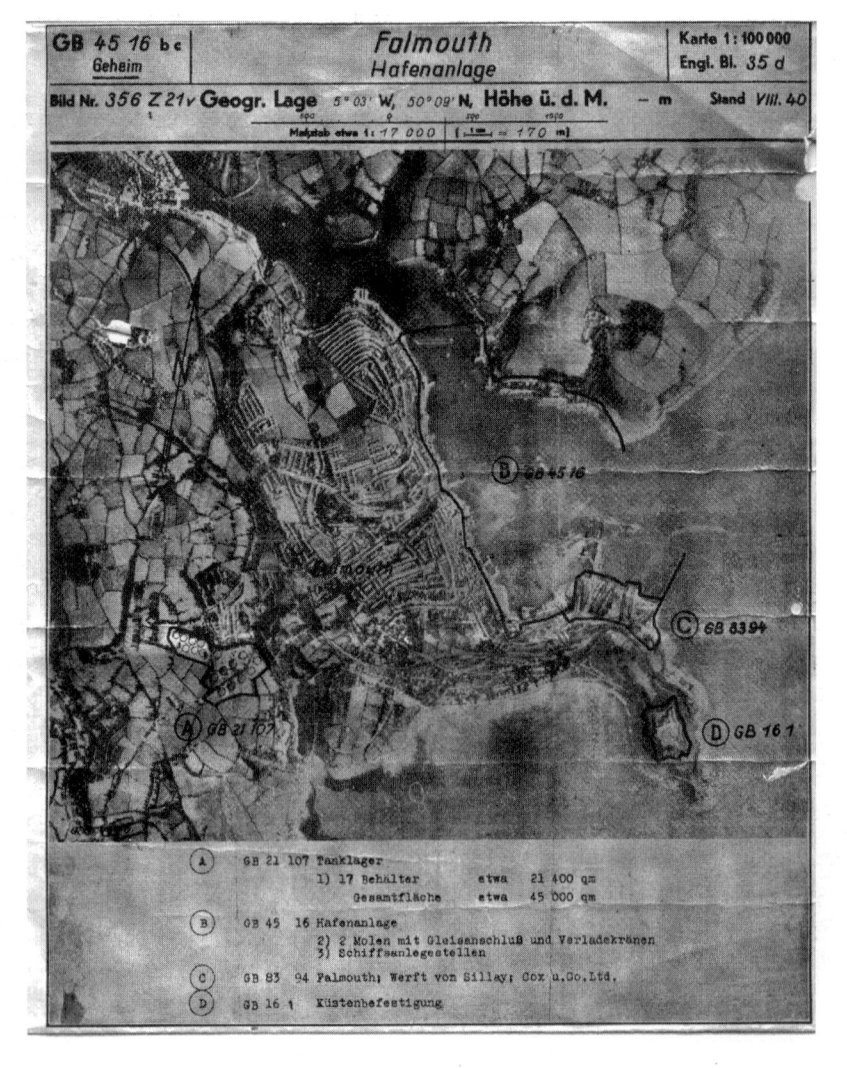

It was while editing the Falmouth Packet soon after my return from the Army in 1946 that I acquired the picture and in May 3 issue of 1946 published it.

It was subsequently reprinted and sold, at 2d per copy with proceeds going to Falmouth Tribute fund.

The picture taken in 1940 was discovered among a large number of photographs in an office at the German headquarters, after the cessation of hostilities, by a member of the R.A.F., who resides a few miles from Falmouth, and gives some idea of the amazing knowledge possessed by the Nazis of the locality. It will be recalled that during the war the traitor, William Joyce ("Lord Haw-Haw"), in one of his broadcasts, declared that the Germans were aware of the site of the oil tanks at Swanvale and were "going to get them."

They made several attempts, but were not successful until the last raid on the town, when two tanks were set alight and the contents destroyed. The fact that such little damage was done to important naval and military objectives is a tribute to the splendid anti-aircraft barrage built up soon after the first raid in 1940, and its gradual increase in efficiency and strength.

The heading and the information at the bottom of the picture, also the lines denoting the situation of the oil tanks at the Docks were printed in red on the original map.

The following is a translation of the German words printed on the photograph: Hafenanlage - Plan or lay-out of harbour. Karte - Map. Geheim - Secret. Bild Nr. - Negative number. Geogr. Lage. - Geographical position. Hohe u.d.M. - Height above sea level. Masstab etwa - Scale. about. A. - Tanklager Storage tanks. 17 tanks etwa 21,400 qm - About 21,400 square metres. Gesamtflache - Total area. etwa 45,000 qm - About 45,000 square metres. B G.B. 45 16 - Lay-out of harbour. (2) Two piers with railway junctions (sidings?) and loading cranes. (3) Landing places (moorings) for ships. C. - G.B. 83 94 - Dockyard of Silley Cox and Co. Ltd. D. - GB 16 1 - Shore defence (or fortification).

Luftwafte pilots frequently referred to Falmouth as Hell's mouth because of the difficulty of finding their targets due to the number of rivers and headlands in the area.

May 3rd 1946

Falmouth's first air raid

First links with the subject of this week's interview were made many months ago when he telephoned to discuss references in a previous article on naval vessels. As a result of that and further conversations, I classified him a naval historian and added his name to a list of future possible contacts.

During an interesting three hour discussion recently we talked about naval and church history and life in Falmouth during the Second World War.

Mr T E (Tom) George, of Polwithen Road Penryn, was born in Hackney, but on January 16 1938, because of family links, came to live in his father's native village of Flushing. Mr George senior was a shipwright at the docks.

Tom had previously passed an examination to attend the Bluecoats School in West Sussex, but instead attended St Peter's School in Flushing.

After leaving school he worked for a short time as a shop assistant then did clerical work for a firm of solicitors and was subsequently employed in an office associated with the building trade. In 1970 he joined the Civil Service, where he worked until his retirement in 1990.

It was in 1937, while in London, that he became interested in the Royal Navy. A newspaper article about the Fleet review aroused his interest then, when he moved to Flushing and saw vessels, including naval craft in port, his enthusiasm was fired. Previously he had only seen the sea once - at Southend!

In 1943 he applied to join the Royal Navy, but sadly was found to be medically unfit. However, his interest remained undimmed, and today he is an authority on the service, possessing a variety of books and documents.

He became an associate member of the local branch of the Royal Naval Association, his particular responsibility being the arrangement of sporting fixtures when naval ships visited the port

This was possible because at the end of the war he became secretary of Flushing AFC from 1946-50, then secretary of Falmouth and District Football League for six or seven years.

At the time the RN Association chairman was Lt Cmdr Dobson and secretary Capt Moloney, a former Capt-Supt of the dockyard at Calcutta during the war.

He recalled that in 1954 the Home Fleet visited Falmouth and he took three half days off work to arrange recreational fixtures. They used Penryn RFC ground and *HMS Battleaxe* (the original ship of that name) put a rugby team ashore which beat a team from the rest of the fleet. Another day they went to RAF St Mawgan where hockey, soccer and rugby were played. A team from a submarine defeated an RAF side.

At Flushing the family lived in New Quay House. On May 13 1941, at 4am, a bomb fell on nearby rocks (the tide was out). The house was damaged and the family was evacuated to Trefusis Cottage. The house at New Quay which the family occupied for 13 years, was not lived in again until 1946.

Mr George recalled that a Mr Morley Cox, who worked in W H Smith's shop and with whom he travelled to and from Falmouth in the Flushing Ferry, had had every pane of glass blown out of his home by the same bomb.

For the whole of the war Mr George lived in the area and he has many vivid memories of those years.

He remembered the first raid of the war on July 5 1940.

He had left his work and boarded the ferry to go home for lunch. Kelly Kessell was running the ferry. 'We went off a bit late. Looking up towards Penryn we saw a plane. A Dutch naval vessel in the harbour started firing and the plane dropped bombs which missed the docks. It then swerved away. Thereafter, according to popular belief, every plane that came over Falmouth got shot down!'

Mr George confirmed a belief that the Falmouth area had more air raid warnings than any other town in Britain.

He remembered a balloon site at Flushing, operated by 959 Squadron RAF, how the Odeon and Grand cinemas were closed to the public and used to accommodate escapees from the Nazis in Europe. There were long queues waiting to enter. Then, one day in April of 1940, they awoke to find the harbour full of Norwegian whalers, for Norway had been invaded. From December 1943 until July or August 1944 (during which time D-Day took place) the Falmouth area was virtually sealed off and letters going out were subject to censorship.

The last raid of the war was when oil tanks above Swanvale were hit. 'I was fearful about that. The wind blew from the south west and parts of Falmouth were obscured by smoke from the burning tanks but the raiders never came again.'

At about that time Allied aircraft were carrying out daylight raids over France and planes would return, sometimes damaged, low over the town.

Prior to D-Day the harbour was full of American landing craft and he remembered the small craft charging furiously around 'as if they were at Brooklands'.

Another memory was of the screaming bombs and of the July day when a tanker and another vessel were hit and set on fire.

Two curious incidents will always remain in Mr George's mind. One misty day three planes came in low from the direction of the bay then when over Falmouth, broke formation, yet no bombs were dropped. On another occasion a solitary plane which he saw, and which he claims had red white and blue markings, flew low over Falmouth and dropped bombs. He has often wondered about these events.

Mylor was also bombed and, while it all happened nearly half a century ago, memories of those war days are as clear now as if they happened yesterday. In 1946 the Daily Mirror published a panel under the heading 'My Friends in Sweden', appealing for penfriends. On an impulse, Mr George wrote and received a reply from a young lady in Norrkoping. She was Maj Gudrun Strandberg of Lulea - 125 miles from the Arctic Circle. The correspondence continued and two years later Mr George went to Sweden. They now have three children - Rolf of Chepstow, Sonja of Falmouth and David of London, and three grandchildren.

The younger son, David, might be said to have fulfilled his father's ambition for he spent five-and-a-half years as a gunner in the Royal Navy. He served in *HMS Falmouth*, *Plymouth* and *Berwick*, being involved in the Cod War and in *Berwick* sailing through the Suez Canal after it was re-opened as part of a round-the-world cruise.

But Mr George, who for many years has heen a member of the World Ship Society, who laughingly refers to 'Turkeyland' (St Mawes) and 'Strawbucky' (Flushing) and who was, for a time, a chorister in Mylor parish church, has a second interest - church history. He and his wife have travelled over 6 000 miles visiting churches. They have been to every Anglican church in the Truro diocese and most in the Exeter diocese, each church visited being meticulously listed, alphabetically, in record books. He is particularly interested in the Incumbents and dates of consecration.

He explained that the only places of worship they had not visited had been on St Michael's Mount and the Isles of Scilly.

It was in 1963 that the interest began. He is a member of the Church of England and the Parochial Church Council at Perranarworthal.

Now, surrounded by books and records and with his multilingual wife, Mr George can look back on a full and interesting life. With an inborn desire to investigate and the compunction to confirm and record resulting from Civil Service training he is the possessor of a wealth of information on the subjects which have taken his interest.

June 6, 1992

A bomb cut our home in half

Two Falmouth sisters had a close brush with death when a 500lb bomb sliced into their home, bored 25ft into the earth missing a concrete surround then exploded, bringing down half the cottage. Yet no member of the family was injured, even two pet dogs escaping.

The bomb, which (confirming a belief) no-one in the house heard, fell at 1.45am on Sunday July 13 1941.

The home was Selwood Cottage in Melvill Road which had been built by Mr Gerald Hick. His sisters, Mrs Marjorie Gregory and her baby son, Nigel, Miss Isabel Hick and their mother all decided to live together during the war.

Falmouth ARP Wardens. B2 Group Headquarters at Sully's P.O. Bank Place Sept 1944

Marjorie only lifted Nigel out of his cot that night at the insistence of her sister, and the half of the house in which they were all sheltering withstood the blast. Isabel said: 'I knew we were not going to die. I felt a guardian angel was protecting the house. Many homes suffered much less damage, yet people died in them.' Marjorie's husband was in the Merchant Navy, Gerald was in the Army and Isabel was an immobile WRNS (serving only in Falmouth) and working in the SDO (senior distributing office).

The morning after the raid the bed in which Marjorie would have been sleeping was seen hanging over an abyss. Mr Sampson James, lessee at Gyllyngvase Beach, loaned the family a tarpaulin to cover the gaping hole where half a house had stood. At 8am Isabel, in borrowed clothing, went on duty in Fort III in Imperial House. A chief petty officer met her with the comment: 'We had an awful night last night. A house up the road was hit and three people were killed.' She shocked him by putting him right, then the medical officer saw her and granted her 48 hours' compassionate leave

She said that for weeks afterwards she had difficulty sleeping. She could hear her sister screaming and the baby whimpering.

Air raid 30 May 1944 - Melvill Crescent, Houses near shelter

Marjorie's home was in Marlborough Road - a house that in 1943 was hit by 11 incendiary bombs. All were put out.

Isabel later became a mobile WRNS member, moving to Yeovilton, Plymouth, Liverpool and Teignmouth.

Gerald's wife and her young son, John, moved to where her husband was stationed, following him around the country.

Marjorie's husband spent 23 years in the Merchant Navy, then after the war 27 years as a Trinity House pilot.

In May 1942 his ship the *City of Melbourne* was torpedoed and he spent nine days in one of three open boats, eventually reaching Barbados where they rested for six weeks. Ken Gregory, who died ten years ago at the age of 76 was a chief officer with Ellerman Lines. Isabel was sent to *HMS Heron* at Teignmouth, a training establishment for aircraft pilots and there experienced some heavy air raids. In one of these the best man at Marjorie's wedding, Jimmy Skinner of Falmouth and his wife, died.

Marjorie has two sons and a daughter. Nigel is a headmaster in Papua New Guinea. Mrs Camilla Blunden is an actress in Australia and Gavin a solicitor in Devon. The two sisters are daughters of Mr and Mrs John Hick of High Street, Falmouth. They have one brother, Gerald.

Air raid 30 May 1944 - Shelter which saved lives of 26 persons

Isabel attended Surrey House private school run by Madame Cliff in Marlborough Road. A Miss Adam was the assistant. Marjorie went to the old Board (Trevethan) School where Miss Burt was head teacher and Miss Kelway a teacher. Finally both girls attended Falmouth High School while their brother became a pupil at Falmouth Grammar School.

Their father, John, kept a china shop with his father Mr John Colman Hick, who died at the age of 84. Their father was invalided out of the Grenadier Guards and died on September 11 1919. Their mother lived on to the good old age of 95, finally passing away in April 1977. She came from St Austell but when the couple were married in 1909 they moved to Falmouth.

The two sisters recently reminisced to me about High Street (a very busy street) in bygone days. Isabel, who explained the three children had been born there, remembered the days when she was about five years of age. There were Head the grocer, an antique shop run by a Mr Helman ('a dear old gentleman'). Their father's land ran down to the foreshore and she remembered her mother telling her that two old cottages once stood below them. In one lived an aged lady who smoked a clay pipe and Isabel's grandfather would give her 'baccy'. Her grandfather built six cottages, known as Sea View Cottages, using stone from the original two as foundations. In one of the cottages was an Adam fireplace. This was sold to Mr Helman for either 30/- or 35/-!

Further down the street was Malins Hall and near there lived three old ladies known as Faith, Hope and Charity. They sold buttons and haberdashery and lived in great poverty. Her mother had seen the father of the three shaking mats outside their house at 5.30am. Two eventually died, but the third ended her days in Budock House, reaching the age of 98. When visiting a friend there Miss Isabel Hick was recognised by the old soul, who was then over 90, and chatted with her.

She recalled that the three sisters attempted to befriend children, though only succeeded in frightening them.

Then there was W D Thomas who sold rugs and canvas, Smith's grocers, Lawrence barber who had a traditional barber's pole outside, Harris jeweller and on the opposite side Wills' eating house, now a wine bar. Isabel has two memories of the establishment. She was thrilled to hear her first ever musical box there. In the kitchen was a huge range in front of which sat a Miss Bishop in white apron with a pet goose on her lap! Isabel subsequently confirmed that the goose had been a pet and had never been eaten!

Mr and Mrs Lawry ran a sweet shop, Jane a cycle shop, Mr Langman (a seagoing engineer) ran Greenbank Laundry, then there was Sawle's sweet and tobacco shop, Pitt the butcher, Eathorne on the corner of Webber Street, selling fruit and groceries. A son was Alfie Eathorne. Jenkins' dairy sold delicious ice cream.

Other memories are of Savage's restaurant in the main street, Andrew's bakery (opposite Boots), Hosking the chemist (by Andrew's), the West End stores with the fascinating cash containers which were propelled on wires across the store, the Falmouth Packet premises at Market Strand (with shop manager Miss Paine) and the King's Hotel.

They remembered their grandfather had had a pony and trap and did a country round to Budock, Mawnan etc. selling china. The pony was named Tommy. Huge baskets contained china, separated by red cloth. and on one occasion their brother fell asleep, was brought home in one of his baskets but was in trouble for he had lost his new cap.

Another nostalgic memory was of the lamplighter cycling around using a long pole to light the gas lamps.

Their mother told them how she used to hear the clump of men's boots as workmen walked from Penryn to work in the docks. Baskets containing lunches were carried on the buses.

They recalled the Mission room on the Moor, at the bottom of Killigrew, where Mr F J Bowles, a former mayor, was a lay preacher, assisted by Mr Gosden who lived in Flushing.

Miss Hick and her mother kept the Castle Beach Guest House (now demolished) which had been built in 1935 by brother Gerald. It was commandeered by the Army in the war and troops were billeted there. After this the daughters and mother moved into Selwood Cottage when baby Nigel was only a few months old.

The much-travelled sisters like nothing better than to reminisce about the old days. They are enthusiastic members of Penryn and Falmouth Old Cornwall Society and intensely proud of their home town, though saddened by some recent developments.

August 15, 1992

An unexploded bomb in Marlborough Avenue

When bombs fell on Falmouth

Forty four years ago the Second World War ended. What happened in Falmouth during the near six years of that conflict?

Thanks to a series of interviews carried out by the Falmouth Research Project there are on permanent record memories of a number of residents.

The following excerpts have been taken from those interviews, in total providing a graphic picture of events in those now far-off years.

Trevethan School after bombing

Mr. P. Winnan
"One Saturday morning the German planes arrived and machine

gunned the town until our Spitfires drove them off. All went quiet until the Sunday when a house near the Catholic Church and homes in Lister Street were bombed. That was the worst for whole families were wiped out. The sirens were going day and night and especially at night."

"I was in the Fire Service operating from Goldenbank near where there were oil tanks. My daughter was with me the night the bombers hit an oil tank. We were standing in our doorway at the time. Something hit her in the face. It turned out to be a button on the pantry door that had split and flew off. Fortunately she was not hurt.

Church Service on The Moor, Bombed Methodist Church in background

Mr. Winnan remembered the day when the King and Queen visited the Docks. As President of the Boilermakers' Union he was introduced to the Queen and shook hands with her.

"She was a marvellous woman. The King had gone on ahead but he came back and joined in the conversation. He said he saw Mr. Winnan was also an Empire Builder. In the meantime the Queen was holding my hand and talking to me. She wanted to know why I was an Empire Builder and my official explained it was because I had such a big family. There were 10 altogether but we lost one."

Mr. Winnan has vivid memories of the Dunkirk survivors coming into the port.

"They were bedraggled. They got a lot of them up to the Recreation Ground and people were bringing in jugs of tea and food for them. They came off ships alongside a wharf'.

One Friday afternoon he was working in a Federal Line ship when they heard a screaming sound and the bombs came down. They hit the water near the Eastern breakwater.

Train bombed in cutting near Falmouth

Miss I. Hick.

A graphic picture of the port at the time of the evacuation from Dunkirk is painted by Miss Hick.

She said "We were at Castle Beach house and it was the most wonderful sight that I saw during the war. Falmouth bay was full of ships. I counted 300 and then lost count. Thousands of troops came through. They came round Castle Drive and some were sitting in Melvill Road. We took to them all the spare food we had and big enamel jugs of lemonade. We put up two families. An appeal was made to householders through the cinemas to put up people.

Mr George Green.

When the King and Queen visited the docks in 1942, Mr. Green said he took the then Queen around. "We walked round the yard and went through all the buildings and on the jetties. The royal train was in the station. It was due to leave. We had come to the platers' shop and I was with the Queen. She is the same now as she was then — busy as ever and talking away to the men. I said 'We shall both be sacked in a minute if we don't go.' So we had to hurry off. She was genuinely interested in everything and the most natural person in the world to talk to."

Mr. Green recalled the bombing of the docks and in particular a hit on the *British Chancellor* which was on the northern arm. There was also a parachute mine he remembered.

He could not join the Army because he was wounded in the foot in the Great War. When the Home Guard was formed he applied to join but two weeks later was told to leave because the job he was doing was more important

Mr. Green went on: "When they first started bombing this country there were literally no defences. The ships in the docks — we had a gunnery school down there—were each fitted with a gun. I don't remember the size but it was fitted on the stern to fire at submarines.

"A fellow from the Ministry came down and was talking to me when the air raid warning sounded and almost immediately the bombs started coming down. I said to him 'Now you know why we're complaining—no warning when they arrive.' Cornwall's not an easy place to bomb. We've got high points like Castle Point close to the docks. They needed to go up to Penryn then down river and over the water to bomb the docks. It was not so easy getting over the point. We had bombs in the platers' shop and they hit wharf No 3—I think with an unexploded bomb. The *British Chancellor* went on fire and a ship loaded with cotton, I think, was bombed and caught fire. She had to be taken out to the Roads where she burned for days. Another time the northern arm caught fire. '

Mr F.W. George

"It was very frightening at times and we had raids most nights when the real war started. Very often they would fly over Falmouth and go up the north coast and bomb Plymouth on the way out. But they always seemed to come in over Falmouth.

"I remember when the oil tanks were bombed, then there was the time when a plane came over one Saturday afternoon. The sirens went and I went out on police duty. We looked up and saw something dropping. Someone shouted 'That's the pilot,' I said 'No that's a landmine' and I shooed everyone off the street. Some went into our shop. My wife told them to get out of the shop and they all went down a passage. But this mine landed in the water and it was blown up a week later. A Dutchman exploded it and he was blown up with it. There's nothing glamorous about war, believe me!"

Mrs. George: "When they used to practise the commandos would come up over the sea wall at the back of our premises from where we could look over the harbour. They used to come along the passage by the side of the shop. We gave them great jugs of tea because the poor devils were dead on their feet!"

She said there had not been bread rationing but fruit was very scarce. Many recipes were made up to substitute for the real thing.

"One of our girls got married and naturally she wanted us to make her cake. We sent away to one of the firms who supplied us and got some marzipan. That was the last marzipan the firm was allowed to make. We covered it with cholcolate and produced a three-tiered chocolate cake. That lady's name is Doreen Bettison now. Her maiden name was Trenoweth. She still lives in Falmouth and worked for us for 27 years."

Mr. C. Collins

Chick Collins, a friend of rugby captain Cliff Roberts, was in Falmouth during the war except for 12 months when he went away. Of the Dunkirk evacuation he recalled: "We gave them postcards. They would write 'I've arrived safe'—didn't say where—'I am well.' One chap said to me 'Here Chick, come over here, Do you know this chap? It was a boy trom Penryn. He was covered with oil and had been in the water. Then a lot of Canadians came over. The other guys were giving away stuff but the Canadians were flogging it!"

He too has memories of early bombing raids on the docks.

"The only warning we got was from a chap up in the watchtower at the castle. He would be up there scouting for enemy planes coming in and we had to take his word it was an enemy plane.

"He would wave a flag and another chap would run in our shop and wave another flag that cleared everybody out. Talk about run, though goodness knows what they were running from because it didn't matter where you went if the bomb dropped!

"I can't understand why they haven't got in the Maritime Museum a painting of the *British Chancellor*. This used to hang in the docks office. A bomb hit the vessel and killed a number of men. She caught fire and one lifeboat fell on another. The tugs came in and towed her away to near the entrance to St. Mawes. This upset the people there who thought if the enemy saw her burning there they might bomb the village.

"I remember once we heard the alert sound, went to the end of the shop and saw a plane coming over fields near Flushing. He must have dropped a bomb and hit the woods there uprooting trees. He came on right across the harbour.

On another Saturday afternoon the warning sounded and ack-ack firing started—the Wodehouse Terrace guns opened up. The plane went on and machine gunned the Beacon. Then we saw a parachute coming down—we started to cheer thinking it was the pilot, but it was a land mine which drifted across the town and over the water near the present Trago Mill store. A machine gun nest near Taylor's garage opened up, perforated the parachute and the mine dropped into the water.

A Commander Roach who was in charge of the base told me "Keep your windows open tomorrow — they're going to explode that mine". At about 7 pm I was walking home and heard a bang. There was a spout of water going up 60 or 70 feet. I was watching this when I realised there were men in the water. Friends and I made a dash to get a boat but boats were putting out from the town quay. Divers were down trying to make the mine safe when it went off."

Mr. Collins did not thlnk people were particularly timid in those days though he said a number of well-known people moved away. A workmate of his who lived in Falmouth moved to Mylor where a bomb fell on a house next to where he was staying. There were others who moved to Penryn where they were killed in a raid.

Mr. Collins served in the Home Guard near Maenporth. He reminisced:

"Every morning would see everybody going down the road with a rose tree each. They had a beautiful rose garden up there at the Crag and by the time the Home Guard were finished it was stripped!

"Another time we were down by the Nansidwell hotel. We had to patrol across the cliffs to Maenporth. I heard a voice call my name. It turned out to be a policeman. He asked if I was on duty the previous night near the Crag and I said 'yes'. He asked 'Did you see or smell any onions?" I replied I had not done so. Apparently someone's allotment was stripped of onions. We all laughed because we knew a bloke who had a shop in the main street. He had had the onions!

Before D-Day he said that some men who previously would never work at night did this for three nights on end. They were only allowed to work on craft to be used in the landings.

One day a Home Guard friend and Mr Collins were out when they met men of No.5 Commando who had become friends and were stationed in homes near the Bowling Green "We asked 'What's on?' and they said they were 'just looking around.' In fact they went on the St. Nazaire raid. Some came back - others never made it."

Mr. Peter Gilson added:
"To anyone reading these reminiscences who might feel there are serious discrepancies, I would appeal for tolerance. By all means point out anything you feel is wrong, but remember these are only personal experiences from a long time ago - and time does cloud memories. None of these people set out to record a detailed history of those far-off days. They simply kindly agreed, on request, to attempt to remember highlights of the war years."

May 6, 1989

A raid moulded this man's life

Srange, isn't it how lives are changed or moulded by some single event which at the time it happened no-one realised would have such far-reaching effects.

On a Sunday afternoon in the latter part of the Second World War a nine-year-old boy was playing in Pendarves Road. There had been no warning air raid siren but suddenly a plane roared across Falmouth and dropped a stick of bombs.

In blind panic the boy started running towards his nearby home, intent only on reaching somewhere he felt was safe. He rounded a corner and crashed into a lamp post knocking himself unconscious. Workmen returning from the docks later found him lying in the road, recognised him and carried him to his home.

The legacy of that incident was that the boy suffered a disability from which today he is still a sufferer.

A few years later he was advised to find a job in the open air that would offer the minimum stress. He was told he must not climb ladders and should never drive a vehicle.

When that stick of bombs fell, homes in Lister Street and Kimberley Place suffered direct hits.

The boy was Brian Philpott.

Today he is one of the best-known of the town's gardeners and is closely linked with the St. John's Ambulance Brigade.

Brian attended the old Board School, then Smithick Hill primary school and finally Wellington Terrace school when the Headmaster was Mr H.M. Bullock.

Gardening seemed a likely choice and Brian set out to become a professional.

Leaving school he became the second boy gardener in the town joining Rosehill Gardens (run by the council) working under the direction of Mr. Charles Thomas Rowe, head gardener, a man whom he described as a hard task master but from whom he had a firm grounding in his chosen following.

He spent eight years at Rosehill then worked on council gardens in the sea front area then in Gyllyngdune gardens.

Until 1980, when he became self-employed he was employed in various council gardens acting as a relief. He spent two months looking after Kimberley Park after Mr Jack Pascoe died.

September 10, 1988

Huddled under the stairs when the bombs fell

For Mrs. Pamela Hancock (nee Maunder) now of 100, Kimberley Park road, my recent article about Mr. Brian Philpott, one of Falmouth's best-known gardeners, and that Sunday early on in the Second World War when Lister street and Killigrew street were bombed brought back vivid memories.

At the time she was a nine-year-old living at 36, Lister Street, and as she pointed out civilians then had not been under attack in this part of the world.

She recalls: "The air raid warning had gone, a comparatively new sound to our ears.

"We were sitting around the table having tea, my mother, father, brother, and myself, when there was a loud droning of an aircraft approaching very low.

"We sat staring at one another, then I think the terrible realization dawned on us that we were about to be bombed.

"We dashed to the cupboard under the stairs which had been declared the most safe place to shelter, and there we sat huddled together waiting.

"There was a terriffic explosion, then blackness, more explosions and the sound of breaking glass.

"I don't know how long we sat there in the dark, not daring to move, for fear of further attack.

"Then there were voices calling "Hello, are you all right?" Neighbours were shouting and trying to open the front door. We picked our way along the passage, and out into the front street where we could see the devastation left by the bomber.

"There had been a direct hit to the houses opposite what had been a neat little terrace, was now a heap of rubble, and rescue workers were frantically digging, looking for survivors. Six people were brought out dead — the whole Pascoe family.

"I looked for my best friend Margaret Maynard, who lived with her parents and brother Geoffrey two doors up, next to the hill. There was a huge crater in the hill, and Margaret's house was literally sliced in half. All that could be seen were pieces of furniture, and a crucifix still hanging on the remaining wall.

"The Maynards were all safe, having also taken refuge under their stairs which were in the part of the building still standing.

"I saw Mrs Nellie Moore being brought out clutching her young daughter Margaret in her arms, although they were hard to recognize with their blackened faces. Nellie was badly cut, and was removed to hospital.

"We all moved that night to outlying villages where it was considered to be safer, Margaret took up residence at Durgan, and we moved in with my grandmother at Lanner.

"Lister Street was bombed again later on in the war, this time at the top of the street, when Mr. Roberts, Mrs. Moore's father, was killed.

"In all five bombs fell in the, area. It was certainly a night to remember."

October 29, 1988

Philip Lee Bishop with the bulldozer he used at Swanvale. (see also page 125)

Fuel tanks bombed

It takes little to revive memories of the dramatic war years in Falmouth. Publication of the picture on the facing page, showing a bulldozer at work in Swanvale, helping to protect homes from blazing fuel when nearby tanks were bombed, brought back memories of those hectic days for two women I met recently.

Hazel Pearce (formerly WRNS Petty Officer Hazel Banfield), who now lives in a lovely rural area at the back of Perranwell, worked with Norwegian and British minesweepers responsible for keeping the seas clear between Plymouth and Falmouth. She was based in the Membly Hall Hotel on the seafront and, for her services, was mentioned in despatches and received a medal from King Haakon of Norway. Although she worked in an office in the hotel, she clearly recalls the underground ops room with steps leading down to the entrance, set on the left of the hotel looking from the front. The night fuel tanks and Swanvale were hit, she was on fire duty. The chief officer was stationed at the Pentargan Hotel and was injured when it was bombed. The bay was illuminated by flares and the raiding planes dropped mines. Mrs Pearce said the hotel literally rocked when bombs fell nearby, and much glass was blown in. She was able to plot where the mines had been dropped.

The night before D-Day the minesweepers received their sailing orders. 'They did a brilliant job in clearing the sea lanes,' said Mrs Pearce. But she thought some of the bravest men she knew were the Marines, who took messages between Fort I and the docks. Many times they were blown off their motorcycles.

She also remembered watching the ceremony at the end of the war when the American amphibious troops handed over a memorial shelter to the town on the seafront.

Mrs Pearce, Probus born, who joined the WRNS in 1941, lives in Perranwell with her husband, Garfield. The couple have two daughters, one living in Lancaster where she is a university lecturer, and another at Treliske Hospital. A granddaughter is a dentist.

Another woman who will not forget May 30 1940 is Florence Webb of Hillside Road, Swanvale. At the time of the raid, the last on Falmouth, she had recently married and was living in Swanvale Road. She was formerly Florence Kitchen of Newlyn, daughter of a Newlyn pilot.

Her husband Sidney, a TA soldier, was with the Royal Engineers, searchlight section. In 1942 he joined the 3/6 Gurkhas with the Indian Army and was then, as a sergeant, a member of General Orde Wingate's famous Chindits, who were dropped 200 miles behind enemy lines in Burma. He and his wife were married in Falmouth register office on March 10 1944.

Mrs Webb's memories were stirred by the publication of the bulldozer photograph on this page, showing Chief Boatswain's Mate Phillip Lee Bishop of the US Naval Reserve driving the vehicle in an attempt to divert blazing oil from nearby properties. For this he was awarded the BEM (Military) and also received an American award for bravery.

His widow, Mrs P L Bishop of Seattle, recently spent a holiday with her brother, Alf Retchford of Kernick Road, Penryn.

Mrs Webb's greatest disappointment is that she did not know Mrs Bishop was in the area, for she said she would have loved to see the medal Mr Bishop had been awarded. She paid the highest tribute to his bravery. She would also have liked to play to Mrs Bishop a tape recording of a Radio Cornwall interview, given about two years ago to Ted Grundy, in which she and others vividly described the events of that day in 1944.

She watched the bulldozer at work and said the firemen were spraying machine and driver with water to protect them from the blaze. On the same tape, Ernest Benney of Mawnan Smith told how he drove a tractor to Falmouth to plough up the area around the tanks. He too spoke of the flares, of finding a flare canister in one of his fields and how a bomb had dropped in the garden of a house at Crill. He said the bulldozer driver 'had a lot of guts.' The area was a sheet of fire and the whole valley was alight, with trees blazing.

Mrs Webb gave a graphic account of how, on the night of the raid, two planes came over, flying low. They dropped a bomb which hit the tanks. Everything was going up in flames.

She said: 'We went to Budock for safety. There were dark-skinned Americans stationed nearby. We could see the pigeons flying around in the smoke. It was terrible - we were frightened out of our lives. Then the man appeared with the bulldozer and dug a pit to trap the blazing fuel. Eventually we returned home. I was in the Coventry raid and others and here when they bombed the docks, but that night at Swanvale was worst of all.'

She was returning home from shopping on the day the parachute mine drifted over the town. Heavily pregnant, she was carrying a basket of shopping down Penmere Hill. Convinced that the parachute meant troops were landing, she frantically turned home. 'I had a packet of soap powder in my basket which kept falling out. I fell over every time I tried to retrieve it.' When she reached home she was panic-stricken and her knees were bleeding.

On another day a friend accompanied her to Swanpool beach. They were sitting there when they saw what looked like a string of sausages coming out of a plane. That was the day seafront hotels were hit and a number of Americans were killed.

October 24, 1992

A Lucky Shot that saved the docks

The story of that day in March 1941 when a German mine on a parachute drifted over the town and fell in the inner harbour has revived memories of the incident for many townsfolk who were here during the Second World War.

Bert Coles recalls the day the mine was dropped, also a week later when it exploded, killing a number of men.

On the day of the raid he was aged 16 and was on the Beacon near an anti-aircraft gun position. 'I was playing football when we saw the plane, the mine and parachute come out. The mine drifted over the town, but was nowhere near the gasworks. A gun crew realised what it was. They fired and punctured the parachute. It was a wonderful shot. We saw the mine fall into the water. If it had drifted onwards it would probably have landed right on the fitting and moulding shops in the docks, causing vast damage and probably many casualties.'

On the day the mine blew up, Mr Coles, who was about to start his apprenticeship as a boilermaker in the docks, was in the time office

HM King George VI and Queen Elizabeth at Falmouth Docks 1942. The vessel in background is the Registan *requisitioned by the navy in 1940 as an armed ocean boarding vessel. She was named* HMS Registan *and was attacked in the Irish Sea in May 1941. Towed into Falmouth by Dutch tug Goliath, repaired at Falmouth Docks and renamed* Registan, *she sailed from Falmouth with 6 locals on board. Torpedoed off Barbados on Sept 28th 1942 by U332, 17 crew died.*

where he was on a rota duty with Herby Watts. The office was run by Mr G H. Gilson (father of Peter Gilson and a man who remembered every dock employee by his number rather than his name!).

It was about 5.30pm. They were knocked off their feet. Hundreds of numbered tags were blown off the office walls. Just before the mine went off about 100 men had been leaving the docks and many might have been injured by the blast had it gone up a little earlier.

Mr. Coles also told me of a previously unreported wartime incident which now, over 50 years later, can be told. He was aged 17 and in the Home Guard. He said he was on a night patrol going up a path near Maenporth and when near the top of the cliff they heard a faint sound like the purring of a motor boat engine. The patrol was too far from its base at the Crag Hotel to make a report so went back down the path to the cliff edge. There they saw two E boats waiting for a convoy to leave Falmouth. Each soldier carried a Mills hand grenade and the corporal threw his towards the E boats. These then made off at high speed. Later the patrol was paraded before a major, admonished and sworn to secrecy about the incident. In those days there were searchlights on The Lizard peninsula. Mr Coles said an old friend Bill Brokenshaw, who served on the Murmansk convoys, was now living in New Zealand where he had been for 31 years and he proposed sending this report to him.

A Falmouth woman who has a very personal and poignant reason for remembering the incident is Esme Lashmore of Oakfield Road, for her brother in-law, Gordon Jose, was one of the men killed when the mine exploded.

He left a widow and a 10-day-old baby daughter.

Mr Jose worked in the docks and served in a wooden boat named *Sapho*, used to clear mines. Mrs Lashmore's sister lives in Trescobeas Road near Five Fields and had an unrestricted view of the harbour. They saw the plane that dropped the mine then, a week later, watched the huge column of water rise as the mine exploded. 'I shall never forget it. They came and told us later what had happened and said there was nothing left of the boat.' The baby girl, now Melvenna Choen, was recently married.

In the official report of the incident reference was made to Cmdr D H Macmillan RNR, an underwater specialist. Mr J K. Petersen of Flushing tells me he was a personal friend and, in addition to all his naval activities, was a practising Christian, closely linked with the World Revival Crusade founded by the late Pastor George Jeffreys. Mr A W Edsor, secretary to Pastor Jeffreys and campaign pianist, to whom Mr Petersen sent the cutting containing the story, said Cmdr Macmillan had later been made an MBE for his duties as chief hydrographer of the Southampton Harbour Board. He was a brilliant man and the 'mouse' referred to in the story was a clever and vital invention.

November 2, 1991

An explosion like a huge steam hammer hitting buildings

Continuing the story of the day in 1941 when a German parachute mine drifted over Falmouth's crowded streets and dropped in the inner harbour, the official report states that when the mine exploded, killing four divers, the explosion shook the whole of Falmouth

In the Municipal buildings, at the opposite end of town to the harbour, staff felt as if the building had been struck by a huge steam hammer, and fully expected structural damage. Similar effects were felt throughout the town and it dawned on the population just how horrific a loss of life would have occurred had the mine exploded in the crowded centre 12 days before. Despite wartime secrecy, it soon became common knowledge that a number of men had been killed while working on the device, accompanied by an erroneous tale whereby the Vernon men had removed several detonators but had overlooked one.

The bodies of Tawn, Wharton, Roth and Schot were recovered immediately, that of Self a day or so later. The dead men were buried in Falmouth cemetery's war section on Tuesday, March 11, a day interrupted by three air raid warnings. Marjoram died of his injuries on the 14th and was also buried at Falmouth. Sutherland's remains were never found.

Even in death the war would not let these men rest, for a day or so after Marjoram's funeral a 250kg bomb fell on Falmouth cemetery. It failed to explode but the crater produced was 16 feet deep.

'What actually happened to cause the detonation of the mine is a matter of conjecture. No trace of the mine was ever found. At the time Vernon experts concluded it had been acoustic, and that the Kango hammers in the minesweeper had not been working properly.

With the benefit of hindsight, this may not have been the case. German mine design (and British for that matter) was always in a state of flux, and while the basic features of a mine remained the same, methods of activation, booby traps, etc., were constantly being changed.

The well known German ability to produce intricate mechanisms was exploited to the full. Among the various systems ftted were 'period delay mechanisms', which delayed the detonation until a predetermined number of activations had occurred, usually 9, 12 or 15. A 'rendering active mechanism' delayed activation underwater for up to 6 hours, 6 days or 12 days. Another device made the mine alternatively active and safe at regular daily intervals.

At the time of the Falmouth disaster Vernon's counter measures department were wrestling with the intricacies of a new kind of hydrostatic trigger, obtained from a defused magnetic parachute mine. The device was a clock driven switch, which triggered when the pressure went above a certain value, usually somewhere between 10 to 15 feet of water. The clock would then run for a predetermined period and the mine became live at the end of this.

A further device had an opposite effect, detonating the mine if it was moved into shallower water, usually less than 12 feet.

Thus it can be appreciated that not only did a mine countermeasures team have to face the main detonating mechanism of a mine that was in 1941 magnetic, acoustic, or even a combination of the two, but a host of other refinements. Refinements which could only be understood by examination.

It was to obtain knowledge of these mechanisms that the men of HMS Vernon put themselves at risk, and in the case of Tawn, Wharton and Sutherland make the ultimate sacrifice. That four merchant seamen should die with them is a poignant reminder of the arbitrary nature and ultimate purpose of mine warfare.

The actual combination of circumstances which led to the Falmouth tragedy are as previously stated—conjectural. The mine itself was probably an LMA (British designation GD). This was a magnetic or magnetic/acoustic device with an aluminium alloy shell. It weighed a total of 550kg with an explosive charge of 300kg. These mines were often fitted with a 22-second delayed impact fuse which exploded the mine if it fell on dry land or in shallow water less than 12 feet. It could be that by disturbing the mine on the bed of the harbour that such a mechanism was activated. Certainly the depth of water was on the very edge of such a trigger's range. It could be, as was often the case, that the mine's mechanism was damaged and by disturbing it some function which should have occurred several days earlier was brought into play. It may be significant that the mine exploded exactly 12 days and one hour after it was sown.

Robert Tawn, DSM, Ivan Wharton, William Roth, Alfred Marjoram, Jan Schot and Herbert Self, are all remembered by memorial stones at Falmouth. On these stones are inscriptions chosen by their relatives. The full gamut of human emotion is here, ranging from the grave of Self which reminds us 'He gave his life that others might live' to a personal message to Wharton from his wife Violet.

Reginald Bruce Sutherland has no such personal monument. He had no close relatives. His name is simply recorded on a memorial at Portsmouth for those 'who have no other grave than the sea', panel 60, column 2. He also received a mention in dispatches.

March 6, 1991 will be the 50th anniversary of the Falmouth diving barge disaster. It would be appropriate at this time to remember the event and those who died. It would also be worth exploring the possibility, together with the appropriate organisation, of erecting some kind of permanent memorial to the men, and particularly to Sutherland — perhaps overlooking the site of the loss.

However, before any such approach is made it would be worth mounting a proper search for any wreckage that may remain. The modern Falmouth chart shows a 1.8m anomaly on a 3 to 5m seabed in the approximate area of the loss. A good magnetometer reading was also obtained in this area last year. A later dive was carried out but difficulties arose due to passing traffic!

It is difficult to say what may be on the seabed. The diving barge was certainly destroyed, however much of the more robust gear would survive the explosion and remain provided no subsequent seabed disturbance has taken place. The remains of *The Mouse* may be considerable. Interestingly, of the four survivors, two, Nicholson and Benham are known definitely to have been on the *Mouse*, while it seems highly likely that the other two, Butler and Marjoram, were also on board her. Butler as Base diver would not have been of use on the diving barge (indeed from Grossett's later comments it appears he criticised the Royal Navy's methods and would thus not have been welcome even if he had a job!). The other survivor (who later died), Alfred Marjoram, is described by Grossett as an attendant. It is logical to assume that the Base diver and attendant, who were superfluous to the operation, would be taken off the diving barge, leaving a minimum pumping and line handling party together with the RN personnel.

From this sharp division of casualties it seems likely that *The Mouse* sank rather than was blown to pieces. If anything of her does survive then the fact that she was carrying such sophisticated and innovative detection devices and possessed a special propulsion system would make anything recovered of special historical significance.

It would seem that no salvage attempts were made at the time.

October 5, 1991

Divers search for traces of 1941 tragedy

Next March, members of the Historical Diving Society, about whom I wrote last week and whose oldest member is Mr. Bernard Breakell (author of "Falmouth at War") plan to visit the port and attempt to recover diving equipment lost in a disaster in the inner harbour which occurred in 1941.

The Town Council and Harbour Master have given permission for the search to be carried out, 50 years after an incident which older Falmothians clearly remember.

Here, for the first time is the full and official account of the Falmouth Diving Barge Disaster 1941:-

From July 1940 to September 1945 Cornwall was subjected to sporadic air raids. The town of Falmouth was bombed on occasions and machine gunned on several with residential buildings and dockyard areas suffering severe damage from high explosives. Hotels and public buildings were also damaged and public services interrupted. The inner and outer harbours were attacked and shipping, naval and merchant, damaged.

In all the raids on Falmouth 31 people were killed, 91 injured and 1,932 houses damaged with 39 completely demolished. There were, of course, a great number of air raid alerts, 783 in all, and while only a few resulted in a raid, it must be remembered that all such alerts disrupted normal activity. At the begining of 1941 the raids intensified, placing Cornwall as much in the "front line" as any other part of the country.

The year began in Falmouth with a number of random strafings, including that of a bus. Alerts came daily sometimes twice or even three times and at all hours of the day and night. In early February a stick of six HE bombs dropped in the sea between Falmouth docks and St. Anthony Point and on the 19th a second raid caused considerable damage at the docks and on Castle Drive.

On Saturday the 22nd sometime between 16.20 and 16.50 a (?) Dornier bomber dropped five HE bombs in the Dracaena Avenue area damaging over 130 houses with three deaths and three serious injuries. Those killed were two women, Mrs. Lincock and Mrs. Elliott and a Mr. Walton. Being late Saturday afternoon the cinemas were crowded, and hundreds of people alerted by the sound of bombs and machine gun fire watched as the black object floated across the town from South West to South East. Reassured by the "knowledgable" that it was a man escaping from the bomber everyone was quite content to gawp as the 600 pounds of high explosive gently wafted overhead, just clearing the gas works, before landing in shallow water off the foreshore of the inner harbour near the lifeboat mooring. The position was between the Kings Jetty and the Custom House Quay and opposite the Albion Hotel in Grove Place (now the Cutty Sark).

Orders existed whereby Senior Naval Officers were required to report mines to the anti-mining establishment at *HMS Vernon*. The Falmouth SNO, Lt Cdr. M. McD. Kennelly immediately did so. One of the base divers Harry Grossett temporarily detached from Southampton apparently informally proposed to Kenelly that he should be allowed to locate the mine, place a gelignite charge against it and explode it from a distance. Kennelly wisely, though diplomatically turned Grossett's suggestion down. Vernon's objective was to obtain as many intact mines as possible, and in any case the type of mine and mechanism by which it might be detonated was unknown.

The Commander (Mines) at Vernon Cdr. Geoffrey Thistleton-Smith RN, dispatched an advance party to Falmouth consisting of Lt. J. F. Nicholson and PO Benham, together with a truck carrying a special launch known as *The Mouse*. This was a craft specifically designed to detect underwater objects, developed at Vernon by Nicholson and Cdr. D. H. Macmillan RNR. It contained detection gear capable of depth finding to three inches with considerable range and the ability to discriminate between metallic and non-metallic items. The craft was also fitted with a "silent" propulsion unit to prevent the accidental detonation of devices. *The Mouse* had proved to be extremely efficient.

The party arrived at Falmouth during the morning of Monday, February 24 and despite an air raid warning that afternoon, set to work. The mine was soon located in 15 feet at low water on the bed of a narrow channel. A marker buoy was dropped attached to a lead sinker (lead to prevent accidental detonation by magnetic action). The position was also fixed by sextant readings.

The situation was reported to *HMS Vernon* and a three man recovery team organised. This consisted of Temp Sub. Lt. Reginald Bruce Sutherland RNVR age 27, appointed to *Vernon* on 13th November, 1940. Ldg. Smn. Ivan Vincent Wharton C/JX 11 38009 and Abl. Smn. Robert George Tawn DSM C/JX 137109 age 24. All were divers as well as mine recovery personnel. Sutherland was a less experienced diver than the seamen, although of course in command. Sutherland, a wartime volunteer, was considered ideal material for a mine recovery officer— he had no close relatives. Wharton and Tawn were both very experienced divers and Tawn had been awarded the DSM for recovering the first magnetic mine underwater at Poole Harbour the previous year. Tawn was unmarried though his mother Charlotte and stepfather Harry Moule lived in Leverington Common, Cambridgeshire. Wharton's wife Violet Annie Sophia lived at their home in Chatham.

The three men reached Falmouth in the early afternoon of Tuesday, March 3 and despite the continual air raid warnings immediately set to work. The base diving boat and a pumping party were handed over to the *Vernon* party. This was the property of Messrs. Risdon Beazley although under Admiralty command and crewed by Merchant Seamen. Risdon Beazley's representative, Mr. J. R. Dent was informed by Lt. Cdr. Kennelly of the *Vernon* party's requirement, and he effected insurance on the several men assigned to assist. These were, William Roth AB Deck Hand, "B.H.C. 9" age 44, married, from Kessingland Beach, Suffolk, Alfred George Marjoram Mate *MV Novio Magnum* (Netherlands) age 37, married, also of Kessingland, Herbert Harry Self Mate "B.H.C. 9", age 35, married, from Lowestoft, Jan Schot, Deck Hand *MV Novio Magnum* age 39, a Dutch national, and Stephen R. S. Butler, Base Diver at Falmouth.

Sutherland dived and positively identified the object as a mine. The parachute was still attached and the mine was lying in soft mud which stirred up immediately reducing visibility to almost nil. Operations were then suspended for the day.

In conclusion with Nicholson it was decided to attempt to explode the mine by acoustic means as it was considered too dangerous to tackle such a device underwater in this difficult position.

Consequently the next day a minesweeper fitted with Kango hammers made several runs at varying distances from the mine. After a whole day's sweeping it failed to explode and it was decided to resume diving the following day. Both Sutherland and Nicholson now assumed the mine to be magnetic.

The day dawned bright and breezy and Nicholson and Bentham in *The Mouse* towed the diving barge into position. Sutherland dived, with Tawn and Wharton in charge of his lines. Nicholson then took Mouse away from the boat along with two unnecessary "hands" (probably Butler and Marjoram, see later). The wind had by now increased but the sun still shone. Sutherland surfaced after half an hour and Nicholson took *Mouse* alongside the diving boat.

The diver reported the mine to be on the edge of a narrow channel in thick mud. The clock and detonater were lying on the underside thus making it impossible to work on it as it lay. Sutherland had therefore made a line fast to the parachute ring and suggested to Nicholson that the *Mouse* could turn the mine over by towing it.

This was agreed upon and *Mouse* and another more powerful motor launch took the strain on a long line. After 10 minutes the boats did not appear to have moved ahead by any appreciable distance.

Sutherland decided to dive again. The diving boat was brought into position and *Mouse* stood alongside so that Nicholson could hear the diver's report betore he took the craft away. It was 17.35. Depth was now three fathoms. Sutherland reported that he was "OK on the bottom."

The mine then exploded throwing a column of water about 200 feet high. The diving barge was blown to pieces. *Mouse* and a nearby lighter belonging to the Falmouth Dock Co., *Queen Wasp* were sunk, and two others *Unebag* and *Richard J.* damaged.

Sutherland, Tawn, Wharton, Roth, Schot and Self were killed. Marjoram was seriously injured. Butler received a severe back injury. Nicholson and Bentham fractures and shock.

The death toll might have been higher but for a motor launch arriving on the scene extraordinarily quickly. The vessel was lying alongside the Custom Quay, unmoored with its motor running. The shock of the explosion threw the cox forward onto the gear lever and set the boat in motion. As the man picked himself up the boat was by an amazing piece of luck among the floating survivors. The men were thus in hospital only 20 minutes after the explosion.

The attempt to retrieve the equipment subsequently proved unsuccessful.

September 28, 1991

An unexpolded Landmine

Falmouth rescue and decontamination squad

These men who were mostly local council workmen made up a team who rescued bomb victims during the Second World War. This is only a section of the squad, because of a mistake in the dates they were the only ones who turned up for the photographer.

On one occasion Mr Dawe, who is in the photograph, had to kill a trapped dog as it was preventing him and fellow rescuers from reaching people further down in the rubble.

Mr Lewarne who is also pictured received the BEM from HRH on 7 November 1941.

Mr Dawe represented the Cornwall section at the Victory Parade and the Cornwall Civil Defence at the Stand Down Parade, both in London, at the end of the war.

The photo was taken in 1945 and is loaned by Gilbert Eddy of 13 Basset Street Falmouth, who has recently retired after 47 years with the Council.

The squads worked in 16 incidents, including Truro, Mylor, Gweek, Mawnan, Coverack and Penryn.

Falmouth Rescue and Decontamination Squad 1945

From left
Back Row   R. Harris, E. May, C. Merryfield, F. Pedley, H. Dash, L. Webber, C. Watts, R. Bolitho
Middle row A. Johns, C. Berryman, P.J. Gilbert, W. Barnicoat, H. Vinson, J. Pascoe, G. Thomas, H. Snell
Front row   T. Trevillion, J. Edgecumbe, C. Dawe, (Foreman) H.E. Tresidder, (O.C.) R.H. Lewarne, BEM (2nd O.C.), W. Maynard, J. Smayle

'If invasion comes then blow up the docks'

During the Second World War many of Falmouth's hotels were requisitioned for use by the Services. One of these, the Hydro on the seafront, owned by Miss A H Row, saw its first service 'guests' in January of 1942.

This fine hotel, built in 1893 as the Pendennis, is today the Royal Duchy Hotel celebrating its centenary this year.

One of the first three members of the 213 Army Field Company RE to arrive in Falmouth and stay at the Hydro was George Curtis, now a resident of Saracen Way, Penryn.

Mr Curtis was born in Whitechapel, London, lived for a time in Kent, near Canterbury, subsequently married a Penryn girl and worked in the docks from 1952 to 1957.

But earlier he had joined the Royal Engineers and they were under canvas in Yorkshire when they received orders to travel by road to Falmouth. 'I fell asleep as we were crossing the Tamar and only awoke when we arrived in Falmouth, near Swanpool. I thought I was in a foreign country when I saw palm trees!'

After service at Sennen, where they exploded a number of mines on the beach, they returned to Falmouth and the Hydro during the first week of January 1942. There they were joined by the remainder of their company.

Their task was to prepare defences against a possible invasion. 'Few

Falmouth Industrial Bomb Disposal Squad - July 1945
Led by Fred Hopkins they tackled UXB's and delayed action bombs in South West, the only such civilian unit in Devon and Cornwall

if any Falmothians realised that four garages at the rear of the Hydro were full of explosives,' he laughed. They had to prepare demolition charges for the oil tanks at Swanvale and for the wharves and dock gates in Falmouth Docks.

They were informed that number three dry dock and the clock tower were not to be destroyed, though they never discovered why this order was given.

From January to September they stayed in the Hydro which, later in the war, was occupied by American troops.

'Just after I got there I met my wife-to-be outside the Grand Theatre.' She was Mildred Robins of Penryn who died last year. The couple had two sons—Eric who lives in Redruth, and Michael, of Penryn—and five grandchildren.

Mr Curtis said that from Falmouth he and his colleagues went to Bodmin Moor for three weeks of endurance tests. They slept by day and walked by night to such places as Looe and Camelford. He was very tired when he boarded a train one day at Grampound Road to travel to Penryn. He fell asleep and awoke in a siding at Penzance! Friendly cleaners put him on a train for Truro, from where he walked to Penryn.

Later he and his wife went to live at Hythe in Kent. Prior to their marriage Mr Curtis took his prospective wife to Kent. At Sandling they were informed she could not enter what in wartime was a prohibited area. Quickly Mr Curtis told the official who stopped them: 'We are going to be married'. 'Are we?' queried Miss Robins, who was just 18. They were told she could enter provided they were wedded within three days.

A frantic rush followed, to contact her parents, get their permission and fix the ceremony. They were duly married in St Leonard's Church, Hythe.

Mr Curtis was posted back to Penryn then, within a week was at Instowe near Bideford. There, obstacles which the Canadians had encountered in their costly raid on Dieppe had been reconstructed and the engineers had to find ways to get through them.

From there Mr Curtis went to Peebles in Scotland, then took part in the invasion of Sicily. After clearing mines at Tripoli they took part in the Salerno invasion. Returning to the UK they linked up with the Canadians and, on D-Day landed on Sword beach, Normandy.

Mr Curtis later saw service at Nijmegen on the Rhine, and in Germany. A member of his company was Tom Salmon, Cornish journalist and broadcaster, who was later to become head of the BBC West region. He now lives in Mylor.

Like many ex-servicemen Mr Curtis possesses an album full of pictures and other records from those war years of half a century ago. And memories of those days are as clear as if it all happened yesterday.

February 20, 1993

Preparations for 'D' day

Last week I introduced Mr. Bernard Breakell now living in Falmouth who, during the last war, was a civil engineer employed by the Admiralty here and responsible for much wartime construction. He has recorded his account of those years in a private history because he believes younger generations should know the major role the town played in those momentous days. Here are more extracts from this fascinating story.

Invasion craft at the Empire Jetty - 1944

The main and ultimate purpose of Falmouth in the Second World War was its contribution to the 'D' day preparations and subsequent landings.

In this area this involved the widening of roads and making access to selected sites and beaches suitable for the embarkation of tanks and men for the assault into Normandy.

He recalls when two brand new bulldozers (TD 6s) were sent to Falmouth to help carry out grading of the beaches.

"Harvey's Yard Beach at Falmouth where we were constructing grids was the venue for our first operational disaster. Grading had to be carried out when the tide was at its lowest. With our new bulldozer— like a present from Heaven —I was down on the beach encouraging the operatives and all was going well until I gave instructions for one extra push. Away went the machine into the mud and tide. It was stuck and we could not retrieve it. We managed to save the driver and wrap hawsers around the machine and buoy it to show its position.

"On this particular day we had a visiting Civil Engineer from Plymouth on a "fact finding mission". He was viewing the situation from the old submarine pier which overlooked the full site. I was called into the office at the Imperial Hotel and taken to task in no uncertain terms and threatened with exclusion from the Department. This did not worry me too much because the engineer was a temporary officer, and I was very permanent.

"That afternoon I went into Falmouth docks and asked to see Capt. Bartlett, Managing Director of the Falmouth Docks Engineering Co. We had become close associates. He called in Mr. A. E Underwood, his Civil Engineer and General Assistant. The next high water was at 6 the following morning. "Right," said the Captain, "Put our mooring lighter over the spot and get that bulldozer up and deposit it on Custom House Beach." The machine was beached by 6.20 a.m. We had no charge from the Falmouth Docks & Engineering Co. Ltd., only a note saying "Consider it a favour well done!"

"Development of the embarkation Hard at Polgwidden, Helford, produced more problems.

"At six o'clock one beautiful evening we were due to drive steel piles into the sea bed at low water. Time was restricted. We had the Falmouth Docks Co. barge with pile driver upon it and operated by docks operatives experienced in this type of work. I and my assistant in charge of the operation were a little late arriving at the site and we took a short cut through woods towards the beach.

"Suddenly we heard aircraft approaching. They swooped over the site and we heard four bombs almost on target. It was at that stage we realised we had been spotted as a potential target by the Luftwaffe. Fortunately no damage was done, but the workmen on that barge who had no protection were very unhappy!

"We were instructed to provide a water supply to the Helford pontoons as quickly as possible—laying pipes from whatever source and overland if necessary.

"My Chief came down from Plymouth and a conference was held at Naval Headquarters. We had planned an overland route for our water main from Kergilliack, just outside Falmouth, across fields through Budock, Bareppa and Mawnan Smith. The powers that be gave their approval of our scheme, and we were instructed to contact the Local Authority's Water Engineer. He would not co-operate and proved most obstructive.

"However, within four hours we were in the water engineer's office.

Our Capt. M. read the King's Realm Act to him and within half an hour we emerged with full powers to proceed. I glanced back and saw the engineer a broken man. I felt so sorry. His little world had collapsed around him. Our Capt M. was really devastating when he wanted something, and of course he had the power.

Invasion craft in dry dock

"The Water Works were handed back to the engineer unharmed within two months of our acquisition of the system. In an effort to speed up the operation we had decided to use six inch diameter steel tubing with clamp on victaulic joints as used by the Fire Brigades. Within days we were receiving lorry loads of tubing all to be unloaded and spaced out across the prescribed route. We went across open fields and sometimes tucked the tubing tight into the bases of hedges—all driven in with purpose made mild steel spikes.

"We had a specially selected gang to carry out this operation. They had to work all the daylight hours that they physically could. The whole job was completed within one month.

"Within another week the Helford site was besieged with Landing Craft on the seaward side and tanks and all sorts of vehicles lined up on the roads running down to the beach. The approach of 'D' Day was near.

"A lot of public relations work had to be done to enable this operation to run as smoothly as possible. People whose land or fields we had to cross were asked for their co-operation, told that any inconvenience was regretted and that any damage to property would be compensated. The whole communities of the villages mentioned seemed to sense that this was part of the war effort. I cannot recall one word of reproach or opposition to our mission. The Helford (Polgwidden) site was an ideal situation for our ultimate purpose, obviating crossing Falmouth Bay.

"Our commission was to prepare two other sites as well, one at Polgerran (Tolverne) and the other at Turnaware Point. Both had been surveyed and deemed adaptable.

January 3, 1990

US landing craft at Grove Place in 1943

A few hours of isolation cooled hot tempers

In this final instalment extracted from his story of the war days at Falmouth, Mr. Bernard Breakell, a civil engineer employed by the Admiralty, tells how facilities for landing craft were provided at the entrance to the river Fal.

He explains Polgerran (Tolverne) was ideal beachwise and only needed the approach road widening, and steel pile dolphins for tying up the LCTs.

"Turnaware Point at the mouth of the Fal was a fairly easy beach to grade and deal with, and the provision of the steel pile dolphins there was not too difficult, but the access road was a problem.

"We needed a phenomenal amount of hardcore.

"We soon had 30 lorries down from the North of England—but fully loaded with hard core they just did not have the power to negotiate our little Cornish roads, and it became a wasted effort.

"Everybody, including the lorry drivers, became very frustrated, and we finished up with a strike on our hands, unthinkable in war time.

"I had arranged to be picked up by motor launch at King Harry Ferry. As we approached Turnaware I could see my man in charge surrounded by irate workmen, including the lorry drivers. I was soon involved and listened to the petty complaints.

"I arranged, tactfully, to leave the site with my chargeman to go away to discuss the problems with a superior.

"We set off by motor boat back towards King Harry and when we were out of sight of Turnaware, just drifted and talked. We had a problem created by a few wild Irishmen among those drivers from the North West. We decided to let them sweat it out. No way could they get off that site until we returned. Their lorries were stranded because my chargehand had the keys to the road entrance which was about two and a half miles from the beach. The only access to the site was by motor boat.

"It must have been like living on a desert island! We returned about 3.30 pm to find the isolation had worked, a day's pay had been lost and our decision to dispense with the lorries and drivers had been arranged.

"Our transport problems for hardcore and the like were also resolved, and the work proceeded.

"For people like myself, who needed a car in order to carry out his job, driving at night was a nightmare, to be avoided as much as possible. We had to use slotted diffused shades fitted over the car headlights. It was really unsafe to drive in such conditions, but sometimes very necessary.

"There were no road signs to guide one, for these had been removed so as not to help fifth columnists. We had to grope our way around in a 'stop and start' operation aided by a road map and compass. Second time around was always easier! At this stage of the war it was unwise to ask one's way as a stranger in any particular area was under suspicion. Fortunately my official passes helped.

"Another continual concern was the fuel shortage. I had been allocated a monthly ration of petrol coupons from Devonport which barely proved sufficient. I applied to have my ration increased and it was refused. I had such an enormous area to cover, it became impossible.

"One morning I saw Capt M. and explained my concerns to him. He immediately instructed his secretary to allow me an additional 20 gallons per month. If I had any further problems I was to approach his secretary again. I was not to be held up—he knew it—and I knew it.

"Of course there were others fighting the war besides the Naval Command and adjacent resources. In these reminiscences my naval connections are bound to be predominant but not I hope at the expense of our Allied Forces.

"We had weekly conferences with the U.S. Naval Amphibious base at the Beacon, similarly with the Army Representation at the Castle (Pendennis) and Place House near St. Anthony, and with the R.A.F. based at the Gwendra Hotel. Sometimes our paths crossed, but never in conflict and each faction had great respect for the other.

"Falmouth Docks was playing a great part too. Almost all the time the docking facilities were full of the smaller industrious R.N. ships such as Mine Layers, Mine Detectors and Mine Sweepers. Now and then we would see larger vessels of the Fleet perhaps calling for bunkering, emergency repairs or a welcome night ashore for officers and crew.

"There was also a faction from the Royal Netherlands Navy. They were based at Enys near Penryn. They were a friendly group and I was in touch with them quite a few times. They appeared to be happy in a monastic sort of existence and seemed to want to keep themselves to themselves. Then there was a small presence of the "Free French" working secretly in a small creek off the Helford River. This was a very worthwhile unit. The "Hard" constructions at Tolverne, Turnaware and Helford were contracted out to "Harbour and General Works Ltd" of London, strictly supervised by my statf because it was carried out on a "cost plus basis". The work on the "Grids" at Harvey's Yard and Mylor was carried out by E. Thomas and Son, the old original firm together with a lot of ancillary works which we knew this firm could accomplish without too much trouble. We had almost taken over the firm of J. Curtis and Son, Penryn. They had an excellent type of workman. It was from these lads that we selected our special teams for emergency works at the "Q" sites and also the water supply to the Helford Hard. J. Curtis and Son also carried out a lot of work for us in the way of small individual contracts.

"Another building firm which helped us with general items of maintenance at various properties taken over by the Admiralty was "Strongmans" (1940) Ltd.

"General co-operation was given by the Falmouth Docks and Engineering Co. Ltd. Without them and their facilities life would have been very difficult.

"My other activities away from the Falmouth area involved a regular team of builders in Fowey, Newlyn and Gerrans.

"Finally I feel that Falmouth, a very important little town, has undersold itself and is worthy of more credit than it receives in any other part of the country. I have revealed a little of what went on from 1939-45. I could not have spoken or written about this previously.

"Falmouth is forever, and I do hope that the younger generation will absorb the spirit of their forebears because they were a stubborn, proud and fighting breed. I am not a Falmothian, but I have mixed and worked with them. We got along alright and we learned great respect for one another. I now feel that I am one of them and proud of it."

Mr Bernard Breakell's story of the war days has prompted two readers to write. Mrs B. R. Lorentzen (ex-leading Wren Kneebone) of Chy Nampara, Trevethan, Falmouth, and ex-leading Wren Allen, a switchboard operator at Fort IV tell me. "We have read the articles written by Bernard Breakell with great interest. He has left out quite a few accommodations that were used by the Forces. We thought your readers might be interested to know that the offices at the Town Quay Chambers (Fort III), were Duty Offices for shipping. There were pay offices, signals and switch-board operators connecting ships in the Carrick Roads.

"Opposite, Bank House housed the sailors who manned the small harbour launches, Arwenack Manor House the Air-sea rescue crews, Royal Duchy Hotel the American sailors and Cliff House as well as

Carthion, Wrens. South Cliff (now flats) Wren officers and sick-bay for Wrens. Green Bank Hotel, American Naval officers. Ponsharden Lodge (above coast-lines) housed boat crew Wrens who manned various launches working in the harbour and rivers. "I cox'ned the no 3 Quay punt as the Trot-boat for coastal forces, (MTBs MGBs MLs Masbies and harbour defence launches). Coast lines was known as Fort IV.

"The coastal forces have formed a Coastal Forces Veteran Assn. and are active all over the British Isles and in various parts of the world, Canada, Australia and South Africa etc. I am proud to be a member and also to have known many of these dedicated men mentioned."

February 10, 1990

Mulberry harbour sections at the docks

Floating tables with four legs

Our regular correspondent 'Nanky' (Mr E Nankivel) points out. "I've not touched on the war years yet apart from naming the little ship Empire Fulham in which I served when still very young. but I mentioned the Mulberry platforms that were anchored in Helford River. They were but floating tables with four legs, massive in size and were used during the invasion of France as harbours to enable ships to discharge men and materials. When in position the legs would be lowered and rest on the ocean bed. No matter how uneven the sea bed, the table would float up and down with the tides. These were moored together and became roadways or docking berths. Few knew they were there, and no doubt other rivers and creeks held more, hidden away. They were manned by the army as far as I can remember. All our rivers were packed with all kinds of different strange craft, from tiny tugs, to massive landing craft, 10 or more abreast. The Fulham was just a little water tanker, but the places she took me and the sights I saw were unnerving at such a tender age. Yet she was a floating goldmine to us, for I'm sure you can imagine all the swag we'd bring ashore from the Yanks who were such a generous lot! And HM Customs were much kinder in those days. If they did know they turned a blind eye whereas now when one comes into port, one can't cough without having a Customs man leaning on one's shoulder!

July 16 1988

Building the Mulberry Harbours

The Treneer family, who farm at Mylor harbour, had a number of servicemen billeted in their farm sheds and on the hill behind. They remember the Frenchmen and how in a very few months there were very few snails left in the area!

Landing Craft on Trebah beach

Pearl Harbour brought the Americans into the war and their contribution made itself felt in terms of both material and manpower. Apart from the increased number of ships, the Americans started to arrive in force all around the Fal area. They were responsible for building a jetty and a slipway at the entrance to Mylor Creek for the repair of damaged ships, and many of them were billeted opposite the church. Joyce Stevens remembers their generosity in sharing food with neighbours from their mess, which was known as the 'chuck wagon'.

Mr Churchill had conceived the idea of creating an artificial harbour off the coast of France to protect ships unloading after the invasion. When the combined commanders were making preliminary studies for a return to France, they received a minute from the great man dated May 30, 1943. It was headed 'Piers for use on Open Beaches' and began: 'They must float up and down with the tide,' ending, 'don't argue the matter, the difficulties will argue for themselves.'

This planning resulted in the War Office developing a massive construction programme to be used in Operation Overlord. The concept included breakwaters composed of block ships known as 'corn cobs' to be sunk in line. These artificial harbours, each comparable in size to Dover harbour, also involved the sinking of ferro-concrete caissons to extend the line of block ships, and included piers to carry vehicles of all sizes after they had been unloaded. These piers consisted of an articulated steel roadway supported by pontoons which were, in turn, securely anchored to the sea bed but free to float up and down with the tide. Planning for the new harbours included the means to protect them, with sites for anti-aircraft guns. The whole system was known as the Mulberry Harbour.

Force B was deployed with headquarters at Falmouth and was responsible for all the construction relative to a Mulberry harbour, much of which was undertaken in the Westcountry, particularly around the Fal. Mr Silverstoff of Falmouth used to be a fitter in Falmouth docks. He helped to fit pipes and wiring onto units that made various sections. None of the fitters or workmen involved in constructing the caissons knew what they were for and called them 'spud columns'. Several of the caissons were built at Turnaware Point, Feock and other local locations.

The US headquarters at the time was located in a small cottage at Tolverne, now a restaurant. Pete Newman, the present owner, states that his parents lived in the back of the house which was visited by Eisenhower. This is confirmed by Gerald Pawle, an historian of note. Mr Newman has kindly loaned us one of the original documents from his records.

Prior to the invasion there was a lot of other construction activity in the Fal area, apart from the caissons. Many slipways and jetties around the river were built for the use of landing craft and ships so that they could be ready to sail prior to D-Day or Operation Overlord—the invasion of France.

Harvey's Yard was used as the starting point for two tank landing craft (LCT). Taylor's Garage, now Trago Mills, was a starting point for four LCTs. Polgerran Wood had a jetty which accommodated two LSTs. Turnaware Point had a long pier at which four LSTs could moor simultaneously. Loe Beach (Polgweddon) had a pier which would take two LSTs. In addition, there were embarkation hards and other facilities which could load infantry into LCTs. All these craft were officially attached to the US 12th fleet, according to the records.

After the invasion of France, Falmouth still played a major role in the trans-shipment of supplies to the battlefields in France and of other vessels, such as minesweepers and other service craft, which were based in Falmouth or St Mawes.

September 21, 1991

Bitter sweet memories for the W.R.N.S.

The stories in "Trelawny" week ending August 31, brought memories of Forts I, II, and III, as I, as a wren attached to the signal branch, worked as a switchboard operator in all three of the bases.

A fellow Wren from those days and myself have wanted any names of local girls who were with us during those "bitter sweet" days. Most memories are happy, lots funny and some tragic ... like the weather remembered from childhood, more sunshine than rain!

At Fort I, now Membly Hall Hotel, there was an underground room 16 steps below ground which contained a plotting room with large maps where ship movements were plotted and the largest switchboard of the three bases. Both these jobs were managed by W.R.N.S. Night duties were split into watches from midnight till 4am then 4am to 8am...bunk beds which were not the last word in comfort! I have many times looked at the now well kept lawn on the left hand side of the entrance to Membly Hall Hotel and wondered if what must have been a Nissen hut was removed when the war ended or if it is just buried...'twould have left a large gap!

Here are the names of some of us who were on duty during the raid on St Nazaire (before and after, of course). Marion Trenoweth, Marion Laity, Millicent Russell, Jane Laity, Flo Trengrove, Peggy Short, Hazel Cane, Genevieve Burke, Muriel Watts, Nancy Everitt, Isabel Hiele and Betty and Eileen Beer. Most of these served at Fort I.

Fort II was also extremely important. There was the mail office, sick bay, transport, telephone switchboard, and many offices. WRNS drivers were kept busy ferrying VIPs, in fact all who needed them.

Conversations of a secret nature were dealt with by using a 'scrambler' line, this being a device which made the spoken word sound like a chimps' tea party, but perfectly plain to the caller and the called. While talking about Fort II every night at midnight a call would come from Ponsanooth, where ammunition was kept in the woods at Kennal Vale. A good Cornish voice would ask for a certain office in the dockyard, nightly the same story..."Hello, 'ad yer pasty yet? All quiet on the western front?"...the reply, "'ess 'ad me pasty, ring ee later", 4am from dockyard to Kennal Vale, "Hello mate, quiet night?" "All quiet on the western front, well so long." Whether or not pasty was a code word or did they truly eat a pasty each night? Question: how did they manage to get enough beef?

At Fort II (where Trago Mills now is) there were more important offices, pay office, officers of the watch who could look out onto the harbour, P.E.O. (Port Engineer), the sentries on guard on top of the stairs...Curnow, a Redruth man, Chamberlain Penryn, and Woon Falmouth - these were ex-service men recalled. Other Falmouth W.R.N.S. who served away included Barbara Kneebone who besides serving at Dartmouth was coxswain of the Trot boat at Fort IV.

September 21, 1991

HM The Queen inspects members of the WRNS at Falmouth in the early 1940s

The role of Falmouth's hotels in wartime

Many of Falmouth's sons and daughters were away from the town during the war years. Stories of the bombing and the activities of the Americans here abound, but just what else did happen in those years?
What role did the town's sea front hotels play? Who was stationed where?

Boscawen and Pentargan Hotels bombed on 30 May 1944

In a fascinating interview with Mr. G. H. Maynard of 21 Park Rise, a former member of Falmouth Post Office engineering department who retired in January 1987 as a technical officer with British Telecom, with whom he served for over 44 years, and for which service he was awarded the Imperial Service Medal, I learnt much about the disposition of the Services during those halcyon years.
St Michael's Hotel entertained officers of all services including Americans.

In Pentargan and Boscawen (formerly Holmlea) which was bombed were Wrens and Army personnel. The late Harry Lewarne, foreman with the old Borough Council, earned an award for helping to dig out wounded people when the Boscawen was bombed.

Membly Hall (formerly Tregwynt) housed the Flag Officer i/c Falmouth Fort I, and the Chief Yeoman of Signals. The St Nazaire raid was mounted from here and it was the HQ of the 'little ships' (ML's and MTBs). On the left-hand side of the front lawn was an underground plotting room covering the Western approaches.

The Bay Hotel was a convalescent home for the disabled serviceman, The Gyllyngdune Hotel housed Wrens and RN personnel, and was named "The Galley".

Southcliffe, which accommodated Merchant Navy Officers and earlier had featured celebrity concerts with Phyllis Selleck and Cyril Smith, subsequently had a direct hit from a bomb.

The Americans were in the Hydro (now Royal Duchy) which was the HQ of the Advanced Amphibious Forces and 97 CBs (construction battalions).

The Gwendra (now an old folk's home) housed the HQ of RAF services in Falmouth while the Army was in the Madeira.

The Falmouth hotel cared for higher ranking officers in transit, plus American Field Workshops in the annexe.

Mr. Maynard recalled that in 1942 he had helped to put in a special land line to the Falmouth Hotel which had to be working by 10.15 am one particular day. Subsequently they learnt it was for Prince Bernhard of the Netherlands who had been visiting Dutch naval cadets at Enys. Above the main entrance to the hotel was the so-called Royal Suite where he stayed. Manager at the time was Mr. Reg Fields.

Mr. Maynard who was a survivor of the Lister Street bombing also recalled other hotels in the area which had played their part during the Second World War.

The Pendower in Seaview Road was the RAF control centre for barrage balloon sites.

Holyrood, at the end of Woodlane, was a camp reception station.

The Greenbank housed the Royal Navy.

Lynhurst, Sea View Road and Tregear, Melvill Road were HQs for the AA defences.

There were four naval forts in the port:
Fort I at Tregwynt;
Fort II Imperial Hotel, Bar Road;
Fort III Above Taylor's garage (now Trago Mills) contraband control;
Fort IV Boyers Cellars (MLs and MTBs - closely linked to St Nazaire

raid and local hero Robert Hichens).

The gun ops room for the defence of Falmouth was at Penhale and Trelissick (Feock).

From Fort III lines of communication went to a barge (YC 5) moored by the northern arm at the Docks and linking all vessels carrying AA guns used in defence of the Docks.

Mr. Maynard said although the events we were discussing took place half a century ago, so indelible was their memory that he could still recall many details. As proof he quoted the following phone numbers: RAF Gwendra, Falmouth 995; Fort II, 980, Fort III, 815; and Boyers Cellars, 1045.

The Gwendra RAF control looked after five Sunderland flying boats (part of Coastal Command) which were moored off Trefusis.

Then there was the Royal Observer Corps, based at the Hornworks, with a direct line to Plymouth. Their reports greatly affected the sounding of sirens and alerting of defences at Church Road, Mawnan Smith; and Roskrow. Two spinster sisters, Dorothy and Audrey French, at the Falmouth Exchange, were responsible for setting off the air raid sirens on command.

He remembered that when 'D' Day had been switched from June 5 to 6 in 1944 because of bad weather he was working at the Imperial Hotel, and so tight was the security that he had to spend the night in the hotel.

Nerve centre for the Americans was at Tullimar and Goonvrea, Perran-ar-Worthal, and it was believed that General Eisenhower had once visited there.

From the houses Pedn Billy and Rediforne in Bar Road, Helford Passage, the naval intelligence HQ operated Free French fishing craft, based in the Helford, across to France. Scrambler phones were fitted there, and Lord Inchcape's yacht was the flagship of the flotilla. The scrambler phones were linked to the Mawnan Smith exchange.

August 10, 1991

The greatest raid of all

What has been described as 'the greatest raid of the Second World War' took place 50 years ago and was mounted from Falmouth.

It was on March 26 1942, that 18 motor launches and five other ships steamed secretly away from the port to put out of action the giant dry dock at St Nazaire - the only dock capable of handling major German naval units.

The old American destroyer HMS Campbeltown *lies with her bows rammed into the gate of the great Normandie dock at St Nazaire. The idea was to make this dock, which could take the battleship* Tirpitz, *permanently inoperative. The destroyer rammed the dock gates at 20 knots. At 11.30 the next morning a time fuse set off the explosives (24 mines & four tons of TNT) in the hull, killing some 400 Germans. Thinking there was a renewal of an air raid the Germans began shooting in the town again, killing many French civilians. We lost 169 dead in the raid and many were taken prisoner. Seaman A.B. Savage, of* MGB 314, *kept his three-pounder gun in action at point-blank range against a pill box and was posthumously awarded the VC. He is buried in Falmouth cemetery.*

The blockade ship was *HMS Campbeltown*, former American destroyer *USS Buchanan*, her bows filled with five tons of delayed action explosive ready to blow up the lock gates. There was a MGB, MLs and two *Hunt* class escort destroyers, *HMS Atherstone* and *HMS Tynedale*. Each ML carried a crew of about 24 plus a number of commandos.

They reached St Nazaire just after midnight on the 28th and with the MGB in the van entered the channel which led three miles up a creek with gun emplacements on each side. In two hours of frenzied action casualties were heavy but the mission was accomplished. A Falmouth-built ML446 got out of St Nazaire, but suffered damage to one of her engines and had to be sunk.

Three days later the company returned—less than half the Naval and less than a quarter of the Army personnel. Among those lost was Lt Henderson of St Mawes. Two officers and an Able Seaman received the Victoria Cross and other decorations included two DSOs and 14 DSCs. Altogether some 300 were either killed or taken prisoner.

Another member of the raiding force who was awarded the VC was Lt.Cdr. S. Beatty RN. A regular naval officer and native of Hereford, he captained a destroyer in Atlantic and North Sea convoys. He was the captain of *HMS Campbeltown*. He died in 1975, but his widow, Mrs Philippa Beatty, and son Tim live in Constantine.

March 21, 1992

A damaged US LCT in dry dock

From the Penryn river they sailed to glory

A resident of Falmouth for just over five years is Mr. Bernard Breakell. He came from Devon but is no stranger to the port. In 1984 he helped to organise a "D" day commemoration service.

At the beginning of the second world war he came to Falmouth as a civilian working for the Admiralty, and was responsible for local civil engineering sites. He was also in charge of preparations here for "D" day.

Now, because he believes younger people of the town should know of its involvement in the war during those momentous years, he has written his story. It is a private document, but he has kindly permitted me to take extracts which I am pleased to publish.

In a preface he writes: "I hope to promote this little town's contribution to those unsettled years which I feel were magnificent and magnanimous.

"During the war years Falmouth was a Naval Port with its own Naval Headquarters and boasted a Port Admiral and full Naval Staff, in addition to having a great repair dockyard.

"So that I can refer back to the changed geography of Falmouth in the war years it is advantageous to promote some sort of a quiz—

"Did you know that — The Royal Cornwall Sailors' Home, Grove Place was a Relief Hospital for British Sailors?

"The Falmouth Hotel (top floor only) was very top secret?

"The Imperial Hotel, Bar Terrace was Naval Base 1?

"The Gwendra Hotel was set aside for RAF personnel operating motor launches for rescue purposes?

"Carthion Hotel was a base home for WRNS?

'The Membly Hall Hotel was originally known as Tregwynt and with its undergound resources was the Port Admiral's Headquarters and No. 1 Naval Headquarters?

"St. Michael's Hotel became a US Naval Hospital?

"The Treslothan Hotel in Spernen Wyn Road was taken over for WRNS personnel?

"The Beacon was transformed into a United States Naval Camp. Their hutments and ancillary works were all imported and built and erected by US personnel with close co-operation from my own Admiralty Civil Engineering Staff who were able to advise on drainage and water supplies. Actually this was a mammoth operation carried out in an exceptionally quick time

"Harvey's Yard off Bar Road became a US Stores and my own department were busy building concrete grids (abreast of the old submarine pier). The grids were concrete piers cast from lowest low water level across the beach at intervals of 12 feet up to high water level. The idea was that LCM'S (Landing Craft-Men) could be beached for a tide in order to have their bottoms scraped and painted and get away quickly.

"A similar sequence of grids was constructed at Mylor Dockyard and for the same purpose.

"When I was drafted to Falmouth in 1940, it was to a little dockyard known as Ponsharden Dock. It was very run down, but the possibilities of improving the situation were immense. The entrance to the dock was demolished and each side of the entrance was reconstructed with facilities for supplying and fixing a new dock gate.

"It was a miserable job to achieve having regard to the fact that most of the work to be carried out was tidal. But, I was used to this, and after a few months we had achieved a very useful docking facility for limited sized craft.

"The main purpose was to accommodate MTBs or Motor Torpedo Boats such as used at St. Nazaire and MLs — Motor Launches. In these very top secret days it eventually became apparent that a base for MTBs and MLs was the idea being formed beginning from Ponsharden Dock to an insignificant but very important ML and MTB base at Coast Lines Wharf — i.e. between Ponsharden and Greenbank.

"It was from Coast Lines Wharf that our little fleet of MTBs set off to rendezvous with the old *"Campbeltown"* to try to destroy the dock facilities at St. Nazaire — which they succeeded in accomplishing, despite terrible losses.

"Our little fleet, sadly depleted, returned to Falmouth and Coast Lines Wharf with great dignity but obviously shattered. I was very proud, and was at the site to see them come back. I cannot enlarge upon this—it was a very disturbing occasion which emphasized that we were at war - with a vengeance. A few more words should be written about this little fleet of small launches, who by day and night set off into the Channel to strike venom and terror into enemy shipping. They were a magnificent bunch of very British and dedicated young men and should never be forgotten.

January 27, 1990

Where MLs were prepared for the St. Nazaire raid

A man who was very much at the heart of preparations for the St Nazaire raid at Falmouth 50 years ago was Bill Hodges, now living at Glen View, Penryn, with his wife.

He is a half-brother of Len Hodges of the Duchy Oyster Farm, and father of Michael, who formerly successfully ran Mike's Sports Shop in Falmouth

Sadly, although he has general memories of his years at Coast Lines, where he was in charge, during recent years, following illness, detailed memories have faded and he cannot now clearly recall the drama of the epoch-making events of those historic days.

He worked for Boat Construction Co, which was formed in 1940 and held the record for having completed an ML in five weeks less than the average time taken in yards throughout the country. During the war the company built 21 MLs and were appointed Admiralty repair firm for light coastal forces at Fort UV, base for the whole South West area. They fitted flotillas for Mediterranean and other overseas theatres and at the peak period employed about 250 men and 30 women. They rented berthing facilities at Coast Lines from where over 40 MLs were operating. In 1942 a dry dock at Ponsharden shipyard was requisitioned and reconditioned. An average of 128 ships a year were handled.

Mr Hodges did recall one man who had gone to St Nazaire refusing workmen permission to board his vessel on their return, probably because he was still hyped up from the raid. Eventually a senior officer persuaded him to allow them to come on board.

In 1945 Mr Hodges received a commendation for brave conduct—published in the London Gazette on April 10 of that year. A proud possession is the certificate of commendation, signed by the then prime minister, Winston Churchill.

There was an explosion in an ML and the ship caught fire. The ship was refuelling at the time and had much petrol on board. Part of the deck and side were destroyed and there was a fear other craft would be set alight. Mr Hodges and another man boarded the vessel and brought out men from the engine room. For this, both received awards. Mr Hodges said he thought the man he brought out came from Truro.

Prior to the St Nazaire raid, Boat Construction Co had to fit to the

MLs additional petrol tanks, Oerlikon guns, special fittings and bullet proof mattresses around the wheelhouses and other points. The engines had to be in perfect order.

While Mr Hodges had no clear memory of the departure, he said he remembered they returned straggling in, one after another.

The wooden MLs were built of the best quality mahogany and teak.

He subsequently worked on the Golden Hind, another famous reconstruction. In later years the company became the Falmouth Boat Construction Co Ltd and is now based at Little Falmouth, Flushing.

March 28, 1992

Wings for Victory gathering outside the Town Hall on The Moor

Eight men returned—as corpses

At the Easter weekend the St. Nazaire Society held their 47th annual reunion at Falmouth.

Mrs. Amy O'Connell, now in her 80s, who has lived in Falmouth since 1926 has her own personal memories of that momentous day in March 1942 and of meeting some of the men who took part.

In an interview with the Falmouth Research Group she explained how one day early in the last war her husband who had been severely gassed in the Great War said "Couldn't you do something to help the war effort?"

So when she was out the next day she called at offices opposite Sully's Post Office (in Bank Place) and asked if she could help.

"They asked me if I was a housekeeper and I said 'yes'. They asked if I could cook and I said I had a first class certificate for cooking. So I was made a chief cook in the Wrens because the chief cook had been ordered to sea."

She lived at home and worked three shifts, one starting at 5.30 am.

"It used to be pitch dark and whenever we had had raids overnight we were tripping against stuff that had come down from the planes. Of couse we were not supposed to be afraid. We were doing our duty for our country."

They were known as Mobile Wrens and were trained mostly drilling, in the Barracks near Bar Road. Mrs. O'Connell was chief cook at Fort I opposite Sully's Post Office and held the rank of Chief Petty Officer. She explained Fort I was the head office. Fort II was at Gyllyngdune and Fort III was an office on the seafront. There were four forts in the port.

She recalled the Dunkirk evacuation. "It was a pathetic time. We had to go down to the docks where we had trollies with refreshments. We gave the troops tea when they landed then buses took them away. Many were terribly exhausted and some were crying with joy to realise they were safely back in England."

When preparations were being made for "D" day she said she knew nothing of what was going on. The only thing I was concerned with was that I would get the food order in every night for the next day. I had 100 men under me at the Gyllyngdune Hotel (I was in charge of catering at four hotels).

"At one of the hotels they captured four Germans who were put on the beach one night. They were brought to the Gyllyndune Hotel and we put them up in a top room and kept them there for a week. The men said don't feed them—I said don't be soft—they're human just like you!"

Her memories of the St Nazaire raid are told in her own words:

"Some of the men were stationed at the Gyllyndune. We had another hotel below us. They used to go out skirmishing in little boats every night of the week. Then one of the male CPOs came to me and said "Look Chief, there is a very special affair on tonight, so will you keep all the Wrens on duty. I asked for how long and he replied, "Until we return to you."

"Eight men came in. Then they went out in little boats. They only had sandwiches. Their orders were to blow up St. Nazaire dock, I think it was. This young fellow who got the VC (he was 29) was so cocky. He said 'I'm in charge, Chief,' and he was strutting around the place—not a bit of fear in him. He said 'I'll blow the bloody lot.' He did too, but he was killed.

"They brought back the bodies of all the eight to a smaller hotel below the Gyllyndune and laid them out in a corridor. They were ringing the relatives of the dead men.

"A naval carpenter who had taken over as an undertaker, as it were, told me to take my Wrens back into the kitchen. They covered the bodies with blankets until they were taken to the naval hospital. They were buried on the Monday morning but none of the Wrens were allowed to go to the funeral. There was a Naval guard of honour.

"Their graves in Falmouth cemetery are easy to find. As you come in the bottom gate walk along the path and they are in the second patch. The man who won the Victoria Cross has this fact engraved on the headstone. I go out every year and put a wreath on his grave."

April 1, 1989

A family link with America

The second World War took place a long, long time ago. We have among us several generations of young folk whose knowledge of those heady days has been limited to hearsay or seeing war films. For all those Falmothians who went away to serve in the Forces what happened in the port during the war years was a closed book.

But this week I can relate a moving story of a link forged 46 years ago between a Falmouth family and an American seaman stationed here between 1943 and 1945 which has remained constant throughout the years and is as strong today as ever.

And the family have named their son after the American.

The story began in 1943 when the US Navy Advanced Amphibious Base was set up at the Beacon. Living there was a lively four-year old lad, David Clarke, who was fascinated by the Yanks. It was not long before he was adopted as their mascot. He was kitted out in a miniature uniform, marched with them on parades, had free access to the camp and always had a supply of chewing gum when it was unobtainable locally!

David Clarke - Adopted as mascot by the Yanks

One of the seamen, Wade Misenheimer, who then hailed from New York became friendly with David's parents and was a frequent visitor to his home. Finally the time came when the base was decommissioned in 1945, for him to return home, but the Clarkes and their American friend kept in contact.

Then in 1959 David was married and in 1966 their son was born. It seemed the natural thing to do to christen him Wade as a tribute to their wartime friend.

They had an even stronger reminder of this friendship in 1965 for

The Americans towing Bofors gun past the Red Lion, Mawnan Smith

it was in that year that Wade Misenheimer came back to this country and in Falmouth sought out the Clarke family and in particular the young man who as a boy had been the base mascot.

Wade has been back three times—the last visit being in 1988 when he stayed in Truro. Now retired, and sadly a widower he lives in Boca Raton, Florida. He worked as an engineer on the equivalent of our Underground.

David Clarke, a painter, and his wife, now live at 13 Grenville Road, Falmouth.

Entrance to USA AAB on The Beacon

While financially it has never been possible for them to make the journey to America they have many pictorial reminders of the trans-Atlantic link. And among their proudest posessions is a booklet produced at the time of the decommissioning of the US Navy Advanced Amphibious Base at Falmouth by the Americans as a record of their stay here from 1943 to 1945. In a foreword the Commanding Officer, Cdr. C. L. Ashley, wrote: "Falmouth may not have been the biggest base but I am sure it has been the best."

US Base on The Beacon

The booklet contains many pictures including the Kings Hotel, the Odeon Cinema, the old Board School before bombing, landing craft on the slipway at Grove Place, the docks with damaged ships before either the Empire, Kings, Duchy or County wharves were built and parades in the town. A number of pictures of the surrounding area are also included in this unique booklet which is simply entitled "Falmouth, Cornwall, England, 1943-45." I wonder if any other Falmouth families have maintained such links with America over the past 40 plus years?

April 15, 1989

Just one year short of the commemoration of D-Day, a link forged during the 1939-45 war between a young Falmothian and an American serviceman has been broken—by death.

In April of 1989 I told the story of how a four-year-old David Clarke, whose home was near the US Navy Advanced Amphibious Base at the Beacon, Falmouth, was adopted by the Yanks, preparing for D-Day, as their mascot.

One American seaman, Wade Misenheimer, befriended the boy and throughout the years the link was maintained.

Wade had been back to Cornwall three times, the last being in 1988. His home was in Boca Raton, Florida, where he worked as an engineer, but sadly this year he died. One of David's five sons was named Wade after the American.

Next year will bring back many memories for the Falmothian who was adopted as the Yanks' mascot. They are indelible memories which he will cherish as long as he lives.

December 9, 1993

Trebah's place in history

Just occasionally a place or a person engender a feeling of living history. I experienced this twofold one evening recently when chatting in Trebah, on the shores of the Helford River, with Major Tony Hibbert, one of the legendary figures associated with the heroic attempt by parachutists to capture the Arnhem bridge in the latter stages of the 1939-45 war.

We had met in his lovely home to discuss plans for the commemoration next year of the 50th anniversary of D-Day

At Trebah on June 16 1994 a plaque, in honour of the men of the 29 US Infantry Division, will be unveiled on the beach below the garden, where so many of them embarked for the Normandy beaches. There will be music, a barbecue and other special events and from May 1 to the end of August an exhibition at Trebah will mark the anniversary.

A wartime tale from the Helford below Trebah has been related to me by several people.

One glorious summer's day a small grey vessel came into the river and anchored. For several hours the crew enjoyed swimming and sun bathing. In those days no-one took particular notice of yet another gunboat. It turned out to be an "E" boat which that evening glided out into the bay and torpedoed several ships waiting to join a convoy! I have been unable to get official corroboration of this story, which certainly sounds feasible.

At that time decoy lights to represent a town had been set up on The Lizard peninsula (to protect Falmouth) and residents on that side of the river all received air raid shelters!

Off Helford, a group of Free French sailing vessels were anchored. They made frequent trips to and from Europe, conveying agents who reported to an Intelligence HQ at a Bar Road house in Helford Passage.

My sense of history was heightened by knowing something of Major Hibbert's career, how Trebah beach had played its part in pre D-Day planning and what stories Trebah house could tell of the internationally-known characters who had been under its roof.

Major Hibbert, whose family home is at Lymington in the New Forest, bought Trebah in 1981 from a Mrs Watts. In 1939 one of the best-known owners, Mrs Hext (known universally as Aunt Alice), died. During the 40 years after her death Trebah changed hands every six years, on average! Perhaps one of the best-known owners was Donald Healey, a major figure in the world of motoring who, in the very early days of television, installed a closed-circuit TV between the house and the beach. Cars were prepared at Trebah for the Le Mans race. Among the house's famous guests were the Duke of Windsor and Mrs Simpson, whom he eventually married.

Trebah was built in 1756 and the Fox part of the house in 1840. A daughter married into the Backhouse family and in 1906 Mrs Hext's husband bought the property from Sir Jonathon Backhouse.

The more recent changes of owner meant that when Major Hibbert acquired the property the gardens were in a far from perfect condition. All the hard work he has put in to make this one of the showpiece gardens of Cornwall, featured on television and in many journals has established the gardens as a "must" for all visitors to this part of the county. Healey cars have rallied there; in June Susan Hampshire made a TV film there; and thousands of people have enjoyed viewing the hydrangeas, tree ferns and other carefully cultivated species.

Major Hibbert joined the Army and was commissioned from Woolwich in 1938. He was evacuated from Dunkirk. In October 1940 he volunteered to join No 2 Parachute Commando. While he remained a Gunner, he was attached to the Parachute Regiment until after the war when he was invalided out. At Arnhem he was Brigade Major of the 1st Parachute Brigade and was on Arnhem Bridge with Lt Col John Frost, the commanding officer. When the bridge was overrun by the Germans and the paratroopers had run out of ammunition, Major Hibbert was captured, but succeeded in escaping after two days.

Helped by the Dutch Resistance, he made his way to Ede, about 20 miles west of Arnhem. He worked with the Resistance for a month and, with their help, "collected" about 130 of our paratroopers, then contacted the 2nd Army who parachuted arms and uniforms to them, for they were wearing civilian clothes. They then went out as a fighting patrol on October 23, about one month after the Arnhem battle was over.

Every two or three years since the war the Major has returned to Holland and for two weeks every year two Dutch girls, affectionately known as "Ninky and Dinky" van Eck, come and work at Trebah. Two of the ponds there are named after them and their parents, said the Major, were "immensely brave". Next year, the anniversary of the battle, he said "everyone will be going over".

A new feature at Trebah is a massive planting of tree ferns. They were brought as dried sections of log from Tasmania. For a week they were soaked in a pond, then planted. Within three weeks they sprouted six-foot fronds —"instant gardening" laughed Major Hibbert.

November 18, 1993

Servicemen return to Japanese attack scene

The Royal Navy has organised a memorial tour in the Far East where two British ships were sunk in 1941.

On December 10 1941 Britain suffered a devastating blow when the veteran 26,500 ton battle cruiser *Repulse* (sister ship to the *Renown*) and the brand new battleship, *Prince of Wales* (35,000 tons), were sunk off Singapore by Japanese aircraft.

Never before had two battleships been sunk by air attack while operating on the open sea and the loss of these two fine vessels dramatically altered the balance of sea power in the Far East.

While there were some 2,000 survivors from the two battleships, many hundreds lost their lives. Tragically an aircraft carrier had been allocated to defend the capital ships, but she suffered a mishap and *Repulse* and *Prince of Wales* were vulnerable to the aircraft.

At 12.33pm, after dodging 19 torpedoes. *Repulse* was attacked from varying directions, capsized and sank. At 13.20 *Prince of Wales*, struck by many torpedoes and hit by high level bombers, also capsized and sank.

The catastrophe was keenly felt throughout the Westcountry for *Repulse* was based at Devonport and included many men from Cornwall and Devon in her complement of 1,309. There were 1,612 crew members in *Prince of Wales*.

Fifty years later a Royal Navy memorial tour was organised. Among those attending was ex-Lt Peter Williams and his wife Grace, an ex-member of the WRNS from Carwinion Road, Mawnan Smith.

It was an emotional occasion for both, for Mr Williams himself served in *Repulse*, leaving her in May 1941 at Rosyth as a leading telegraphist. His brother, John Renfree Williams, died in her.

Peter joined *Repulse* as a boy telegraphist in January 1939 and in 1971 was invalided out of the Royal Navy as a lieutenant.

Born in Post Office Yard in Falmouth he attended the Board School (Trevethan) infants then Wellington Terrace School. He was an *HMS Ganges* boy serving at Shotley.

His wife Grace, daughter of a well-known Falmouth baker, attended Miss Trouson's school. She knew her husband before the war, meeting him in 1937.

They have been married for 47 years and have two daughters -

Lesley, whose husband is Lt Cmdr Keith Brimley RN (now in Hong Kong) and Allison, the younger, married to a lieutenant colonel in the Argyll and Sutherland Highlanders - now serving in Germany.

On October 30 Mr and Mrs Williams went to Hong Kong to see their daughter and son-in-law (their first return visit in 20 years). Lesley was a teacher at St George's School there working with the Services Children's Education authority.

Mr Williams was in Hong Kong in 1945 for the surrender of the Japanese garrison.

A keen rugby player, he captained the China Fleet Rugby XV. During and after the war he appeared for Falmouth and had as playing colleagues John Kendall Carpenter, who captained England, John Williams (High Sheriff), Vic Roberts and Dicky George. He also played for the services with Captain Alan Meredith of Constantine.

The couple returned to the UK from the memorial trip on December 15. It was Mrs Williams' second visit to the Far East.

During the tour the party stayed in Singapore, Malacca, Kuala Lumpur and Kuantan.

The Royal Navy made available the frigate *HMS Sheffield* and the party sailed for four hours to the site of the sinkings. The wrecks, now designated as official war graves, were 200 metres below them.

A memorial service was held over each vessel and crosses and poppies, weighted with bricks, were laid.

The 'pilgrims', as members of the party were described, also toured the Singapore area, went to Kranji war cemetery and Changi prison where they saw the chapel and museum, visited a shipyard and barracks.

They also attended a memorial service in St Andrew's Cathedral, Singapore, where they were welcomed by the Dean.

Mr Williams named the following from Falmouth who served in *Repulse*: Lt Cmdr Cyril Peters, Howard Riddle (of Porhan Street) and Cyril Tiddy, whose father worked in the docks; two Edwards brothers from Penzance and Alec Ross from Penryn.

He recalled that in 1939-40 *Repulse* came into Falmouth Bay. Janner Snell, then lifeboat coxswain, brought a boat out to her, but the crew members were not allowed ashore.

A Mr Frank Fothergill, who was best man at the Williams' wedding and is now living in Portsmouth, was also a survivor.

One hundred and nine went on the memorial trip, which included 14 *Repulse* survivors, some over 80+ years of age. The trip leaders were Peter Dunstan, formerly of Stithians and Tom Fitzsimmons.

In October an 18-year old member of the polaris submarine *HMS Repulse* dived onto the wreck and attached a white ensign to her.

January 11, 1992

'Small cog' with such a vital wartime role

In nearly nine years of writing this column only two people have declined to be interviewed. Then there is another man—the subject of this article—to whom I shall refer simply as "Mr X". He describes himself as "a very private person" and lives in West Cornwall.

But there is justification for including this story at this time. His grandmother was a member of the well-known Penryn Furneaux family and his father was born at Falmouth.

His grandfather, a Belgian, came to England in the 1880s. He was a superintendent with the Eastern Telegraph Company and was sent to Falmouth to lay a cable from Cornwall to Morocco. First the cable went across the Helford River to Kennack Sands, then to Bilbao, on to Barcelona and finally Morocco. Mr X's grandfather went to Barcelona, from where he returned to Cornwall. In 1896 he and his grandmother lived at Helford Passage in Watch House, in which the head coastguard subsequently resided.

Mr X himself was born at Hossegors, near Biarritz. His mother was French and his father was assistant manager of Foyers aluminium factory in Scotland. At the age of three months Mr X was taken by his mother, with his sister and a nanny, to Foyers, Inverness. His father was an eminent engineer and, before the war, went to France to join Foyers. When a student, his father was sent to his brother in the South of France and at Biarritz met and married his mother. This was also pre-war.

My subject went to prep school at Broadstairs, then on to Oundle public school, Northants. After leaving school he worked his passage in an old tramp steamer, the *SS Belltoy*, from Cardiff to Bilbao. There, he worked for E K Earle, brass and aluminium manufacturers. He left for Germany and in Hamburg was employed by I G Farben Industrie. In 1938 he returned to the UK.

Up to the age of 21 he had had dual nationality—French and English—but opted for the latter. Next, he joined Imperial Smelting, a company in the City. This work was classed as a reserved occupation and he remained with the firm until France fell when he joined the Royal Navy at Bristol as a matelot. He served in *HMS Rodney* and was then posted to an officer training unit at Hove from where he emerged as a sub-lieutenant.

Because of his linguistic abilities he volunteered for Allied submarines and was posted to the 7th Submarine Flotilla at Dundee. This was the base for many Allied subs—Dutch, Polish and French, as well as British. He joined the Free French submarine *FFS Minerve* as liaison officer, the vessel carrying out protection duties for the Russian convoys.

At the end of 1942 he was invalided out of the submarine service and joined Naval Intelligence. He was posted to a section in Oxford known as the Inter-Service Topographical Department, which had originally been set up following Churchill's disillusionment with intelligence gathering prior to the Norwegian campaign.

This became the biggest intelligence-gathering department in Europe at that time. It was inter-service and inter-country and all known experts in a variety of matters were attached. The aim was to give the Armed Forces the very best intelligence possible for raids, parachute drops and the like, as well as planning for D-Day Mr X's task was to obtain as many details as possible about beaches and smaller harbours in Normandy.

Although he was still a Royal Naval officer, he worked in civilian clothes, only donning uniform to meet Service personnel.

This quietly spoken, self-effacing man, who, incidentally, also did a North Sea patrol in the Dutch submarine 014, assured me he was just a small cog in a big wheel . Fortunately for the Allies the efficient working of many such small cogs ultimately resulted in victory.

November 11, 1993

The day we drove over an unexploded bomb

In 1936 Reginald Rogers, now of New Street, Penryn, joined Penryn Volunteer Fire Brigade. Twenty-eight years later he retired in Falmouth as a station officer.

From those years he retains a wealth of memories - of the Plymouth blitz, of driving unknowingly over an unexploded bomb, and of a large number of fires in ships and on shore. He was awarded two medals and gifts from grateful ship owners.

His wife died in 1961 and Mr Rogers now shares a home with his daughter, Pat Parsons. A son, Desmond, of Lelant, formerly a senior police officer, is now clerk to Hayle Town Council.

When Mr Rogers joined the brigade in 1936, the captain at Penryn was Harold Curgenven. On the outbreak of war he was moved to Falmouth with the AFS, where the captain was Charles Strongman. Mr Rogers transferred from the volunteers to full-time service. Subsequently, Station Officer Walder took over the Falmouth station.

Reginald joined the central station on The Moor where he was made leading fireman, then was appointed in charge of the North Parade station, where Collins and Williams's garage stood at the bottom of Old Hill. During the war, he recalled, there were five stations on The Moor, at Gyllyngdune and North Parade, with substations at the junction between Tregenver and Trescobeas roads, at Flushing and Goonvrea Farm, near Enys. He was moved from North Parade to Truro where, as a section officer, he was second in command. From Truro he went to Newquay, then joined an 'overseas' group being posted to Lee Mill outside Plymouth. He remained there until the unit was disbanded at the end of 1945, when he returned to Falmouth, where he remained until his retirement.

He has vivid memories of the Plymouth blitz, during which he operated a relay pump from the docks. He remembered occasions when there was a 'sea of fire all around'.

'There was a house which I watched start burning. I asked for permission to take water from the relay to save the home. This was refused because the need elsewhere was greater and we watched the house burn down. An old lady came along and said she too had watched three of her houses burn, then added Hitler wasn't going to drive her out of Plymouth!' One night the men were sent to rest in a house. The next night that building received a direct hit.

One day, when Reginald was driving from Saltash to Plymouth, they saw a long column of firefighting and other vehicles held up. Bypassing them, Reginald drove with difficulty round a crater. When he was asked from where he had come, he was told he had driven over an unexploded bomb. His fire officer was not amused!

He spoke of post-war fires in St George's Hall (which was severely damaged); at Osborne's store in 1962, when the blaze was prevented from spreading; the Falmouth branch British Legion; and Wagstaff's shop. But it was outbreaks in ships which were most memorable.

There was a fire in a vessel carrying fish meal, and he instructed the pilot, Syd Timmins, to put the vessel by Penryn Quay. 'She was stinking and town councillors came to view her. There were many complaints. The fire was eventually put out and the vessel sent to Wales for unloading, a fire crew sailing in her.'

In February 1956 a Norwegian fruit ship, the *Bayard*, caught fire in the Western Approaches. She was ablaze from stem to stern and was towed into Falmouth Bay by the rescue tug, *Turmoil*. There, firemen extinguished the fire. Reginald received a barometer from the grateful owners.

During the war there were many fires in the docks. On one occasion, four ships were on the northern arm. One, a British tanker, was hit, towed off and beached near Trefusis. Another vessel, with a cargo of cotton, was set on fire and towed to near Place House. A trawler anchored nearby wanted to get away, but wires from the stranded ship were over the trawler's moorings. Reginald remembered cutting the trawler free, using axes.

In 1952 breathing apparatus had to be used when the *City of Lichfield*, carrying a cargo of dangerous chemicals and moored at number five buoy, was on fire.

There was nearly an international incident in June 1959 when a German ship, *Ocean Layer*, was on fire in the bay. The captain refused to allow firemen on board and they only managed to board after lengthy negotiations.

In August 1961 the *Madeline*, a Swedish ship, had a fire on board which was put out. Two firemen accompanied her to Rotterdam.

Again in 1961, the *British Fern* was alight in the bay. She was taken to number five buoy where she was described as a 'floating bomb'. The fire was eventually extinguished.

But the ship fire Reginald most clearly recalls took place in 1964 on board the Greek vessel *Stylianos Restis*, carrying fish meal. She was in the bay, then limped to number five buoy. The engine room was almost gutted, but the ship was saved. It was the last day of Reginald's service and a boat was sent out to the vessel to collect him safely.

From the owners he later received an inscribed table lighter.

He possesses the Fire Service Medal and another medal and certificate from the Grand Prior of the Hospital of St John Jerusalem (in England) for service in the cause of humanity. The latter was for helping in the rescue of a soldier who had fallen from cliffs between Swanpool and Gyllyngvase. Reginald recalled that, when he first joined, the 22-man pumper was in use. He was a member of St Gluvias Choir and, one day when Mylor School was on fire, the choir turned out to help push the pump up St Gluvias Hill. Later 'Ginger' Harry arrived with his horses. Meanwhile Henry Passmore, Penryn rugby player, was on the roof of the blazing school throwing buckets of water on the fire.

Reginald produced a picture showing two senior fire officers - Owen Hooker and Jimmy Ashwin - adding that both had served under him as firemen.

He listed those fire service veterans in the area who he believed were still alive, naming William Summers, Henry Watson, Jock Phillips, Felix Stephens, Jack Berryman, Jack Lang, Jim Pellow and John Holland.

November 7, 1992

An impression of Falmouth's inner harbour at the time of D-Day 1944, painted by Falmouth marine artist Tony Warren, some four years ago, for his grandson.

From £9 car to fire engine

If there was ever a medal for the most ingenious fireman, it would surely go to former station officer Bill Summers of Falmouth.

Eighty-six-year-old Bill, now a resident of King Charles Court, was the officer in charge of the Gyllyngdune sub-station during the war, when that crew bought a Daimler saloon for £9 and converted it into a fire engine, built their own watch room and store for equipment and even their own air raid shelter.

Bill sportingly gives credit for the engine to Gerry Andrews. a former stalwart of the Pendennis Motor Cycle and Light Car Club, but it was undoubtedly Bill's enthusiasm and skill as a former blacksmith that enabled all to be done. He said he had made all the fittings for the converted Daimler, which he descnbed as a 'wonderful vehicle', which they had taken to the Plymouth blitz.

He was the son of Mr and Mrs William Summers of Norfolk Road and attended the Board School. He had a blacksmith's shop first in Webber Street, then in Quarry Hill, in premises formerly occupied by Mr Dunstan. Mr Summers' wife died many years ago. In earlier years she was a cook with the fire service.

His grandfather was a member of the town's first fire brigade and Bill joined the force just before the Second World War, when the station was on The Moor. 'I didn't want to shoot anyone, but rather wanted to help people so I joined the brigade,' he said.

He was filling sand bags outside the free library when he was told to open the sub station at Gyllyngdune. From leading fireman he rose to section officer, then station officer. At Gyllyngdune he was in charge of 12 men. And there they had a trailer pump.

He believed the air raid shelter they had built was still there, behind a wall on the car park.

He was at Gyllyngdune when the South Cliff Hotel on the seafront was hit. One evening Gerry Andrew had taken out the Daimler. A raid was getting worse and Bill ordered him to return. The next morning they saw a half block of concrete had been blown from Avenue Road, when Selwood Cottage was bombed, onto the very spot where Mr Andrews and the Daimler had been standing!

During the war years Bill also saw service in Plymouth and London, and later spent some time in Liverpool. In all, he gave 25 years of service to the brigade.

He had one other memory. He said that one of his earlier jobs had been to wind the town clock. He understood the clock, in sections, was stored in a chapel at the cemetery.

November 7, 1992

A link first forged in the War

"Isn't it a small world." How often one hears this comment, yet a recent personal experience has made me endorse the statement even more strongly.

Thirty years ago in Kent, I learnt that a next-door neighbour, who has since become a close friend, had been adopted by his grandparents. He knew only that his father was a Canadian soldier who had been over here during the war. He kept in contact with his mother who lived in Croydon.

About 18 months ago he read a magazine article which told how some families had been reunited and the name of a Dutch woman who had married a Canadian was given as a researcher. My friend wrote to her, then for a year heard nothing.

Finally the woman telephoned him, apologised for the delay and said she had discovered that his father had made one determined attempt to trace him, but without success. It seemed that my friend's mother who subsequently divorced her husband, had refused to go to Canada after she married the Canadian and to prevent him getting the baby boy had had him adopted by her parents, whose name he took.

Her son knew nothing of this.

Both mother and father are now dead, but to his joy my friend has discovered he has three half-sisters and a step-mother in Toronto. Letters have been exchanged and on June 10 two of the half-sisters were due over here. My friend and his wife plan to go to Canada in August.

For me the most amazing revelation concerned Falmouth. It appears that the father was stationed here and suffered a severe accident. He vaulted a hedge not knowing that the road was far below, broke a rib that pierced his body, was hit by a car and lay on the roadside all night. The next morning a passing workman found him. Blood was urgently needed. Dr. McKeirnan collected regular donor Michael Binham of 100A, Killigrew Street who was on duty at the time as an air raid warden and took him to Falmouth hospital where the men lay side by side in two beds and the transfusion was made.

Sadly Mr. Binham died in 1976, but from one of his daughters, Betty, now living in Exeter and married to a son of Mr. Les Spargo who kept a grocer's shop near the Bowling Green, I learnt that since the war days the families in Toronto and Falmouth had always kept in touch. The Canadian and his wife visited Falmouth in the 1960s and again in 1974. They had also called on Betty in 1974, when she was living in Bristol.

Another sister, Anita Eddy, lives in Bournemouth.

The Binham family consisted of Johnny (Portsmouth), Michael (Falmouth), Tommy (Weston-super-Mare), Ernie (Falmouth), Harry (Falmouth), and sisters Dorothy and Elizabeth.

Little did we realise 30 years ago that my neighbour and I had a then unsuspected bond in Falmouth. I am glad that after talking with Mrs. Spargo I have been able to fill in some of the gaps for him.

The Dutch lady who has devoted 10 years of her life to reuniting families told my friend his was the 750th case she had handled!

June 23, 1990

VE-Day Street party, Berkeley Cottages

Another who missed death in *Lancastria*

Mr R A Monk of Portland Gardens, Falmouth, writes as follows.

'It was with great interest that I read from a Mr William Monahan telling of his experiences at St Nazaire (June 18-20 1940) and the disaster involving the liner *Lancastria*.

'I was also fortunate not to be on board the ill-fated *Lancastria*. I was in the RAF, stationed near Nantes, not too far away from St Nazaire. We had orders to destroy all equipment and make our way to St Nazaire. This was on June 17/18. St Nazaire was full of troops, mostly airmen waiting to leave.

'I met an old friend of mine on the quayside, Arthur Odgers from Penryn. We had both served our apprenticeship at Taylors Garage, Town Quay, Falmouth. Arthur was one of the unfortunate ones. He went in the *Lancastria* and did not survive. My unit then dispersed to the town to await our turn.

'The *Lancastria* was bombed in the early afternoon. We saw the bombers going over and heard the explosions. We were told that she took a direct hit. A bomb went down a funnel and blew the bottom out. Those on board had no chance.

'We left that same night in a little Welsh collier packed to the gunwales. I even remember her name, the *SS Floristan*. We heard afterwards that she was one of the last to leave St Nazaire.

'After passing the Cornish coast I could see Falmouth bay. I was hoping we would land at Falmouth, instead it was Plymouth.

'After a couple of days with very little food, the tea and buns supplied by the kind ladies of Plymouth were very welcome.

'The sinking of the *Lancastria* was a great disaster and it was certainly hushed up. I had no idea that 1,500 lost their lives. I knew she was full of airmen.

'On reflection I cannot think that this tragedy could have been avoided, except to embark at night, but then time was of the essence and there was very little of that! There was no air cover. All our planes had left for Britain and our bases were too far away. I saw no anti-aircraft fire. The poor old *Lancastria* was an open target.

'All this happened 52 years ago, but we still vividly remember it.'

October 10, 1992

Merchant Navy Pool memories

In our issue dated January 25 Mr C Pender of Truro wrote of the Merchant Navy Pool at Falmouth and raised some queries about the war days.

Now Mrs Enid Brien of Arwyn Place, Falmouth replies:

'I was shorthand typist at the Falmouth branch of the National Union of Seamen from January 1940 to December 1944.

'Jack Powdrill then came to Falmouth as secretary from Middlesborough, and was there when I left the office to start a family. (I'd married in 1942 - a chippy in the Merchant Navy called Fleming who was afterwards employed at Falmouth Docks, and in 1944 at Devonport Dockyard working on the invasion barges).

'Our office was on Customs House Quay, where 'Harbour Lights' fish and chip shop now stands. The men came up the steps from the quay and we were behind a grille like employees at post offices.

'Yes, sadly many of our local men crews were torpedoed and killed. I remember the chief steward from Dracaena Avenue, he and his wife had a lovely little girl, Linda. I think his widow still lives there; and yes, I do remember chief cook Geoffrey Martin, who came into our office a lot and was, I seem to recall, a member of a well known Falmouth Waterfront family. I did not know his sister.

'A crew from Falmouth were sent to Milford Haven to join a ship around about Christmas 1941, and were later reported torpedoed and drowned. I don't know if that ship was the *SS Leadgate* or not.

'We were not told the names of ships to which we sent crews to sign on in wartime.

'Most of those coming to Falmouth to be repaired at that time and signing on crews from here were from BYC (British Yankee Co), ie *British Commodore, British Cavalier* etc, also some from Athol Line - *Athol Duchess, Athol Sultan* - and some of the Federal (New Zealand Shipping Co) ships which either had English county names such as *Durham, Sussex, Cornwall* or New Zealand ones like *Hococater, Huxunue* etc.'

February 15, 1992

Swanvale fuel tanks hit by raiders

The night of May 30 1944 was one that residents of Swanvale at that time will never forget. That was the night when oil tanks above their homes were hit and set alight by German bombers.

A recent visitor to Penryn was Mrs P L Bishop from Seattle in the United States. She was holidaying at the home of her brother Mr Alf Retchford of Kernick Road

Her visit revived memories of that dramatic night, for her late husband, chief boatswain's mate Philip Lee Bishop of the United States Naval Reserve, was awarded the British Empire Medal (Military) for his outstanding bravery on that occasion.

The petrol tanks burst open and a torrent of blazing fuel threatened the houses. While the raid was at its height, Mr Bishop was asked by his unit to assist at Swanvale. After surveying the situation he volunteered to drive a large earth-moving bulldozer and attempted to divert the flow of blazing fuel onto waste ground.

This he succeeded in doing and, for this heroic act, in addition to his British award, received the US Navy and Marine Corps medal from the President of the USA.

Only three weeks before the raid Mr and Mrs Bishop had been married in the Wesley Chapel, Penryn and were living in Albany Road, Falmouth.

With her Mrs Bishop brought copies of both medal citations.

September 26, 1992

A dockworker in two world wars

There must be few still alive who can claim to have worked in Falmouth docks in two world wars, yet this is the unique experience of Mr. E. C. (Cyril) Thomas of 1, Tresawle Road, Falmouth.

A wood shipwright, Mr. Thomas served his apprenticeship with Cox and Company, starting work in 1917.

He remembers the famous "Q" ships of the Great War— those innocuous-looking vessels that when stopped by German U boats dropped shutters and dummy upperworks to reveal guns. They were responsible for sinking a number of enemy submarines. He recalled the *Mary B Mitchell*, two yachts, the *Rovenska* ard *Venetia*, and trawler the *Rosetta*.

In the Second World War when he also served in the Home Guard he was in the docks when ships were bombed. He remembers the survivors of Dunkirk being landed there and countless air raids.

In 1938 Mr. Thomas helped to build a base for a four inch gun in the aft section of the liner *Monarch of Bermuda.*

Mr. Thomas worked at the docks until June 30 1946 when he left to join Mr. Ken Williams at Thomas's shipyard in North Parade.

May 19, 1990

Veterans' association prepares for D-Day anniversary events

One couple for whom 1994 will see the culmination of nearly five years of planning are Major and Mrs David Preece, of Rame Cross near Penryn.

Major Preece is chairman of the South West branch of the Normandy Veterans' Association, originally involving Cornwall, Devon and Somerset, but now only taking in the Duchy.

He assumed this position four years ago and next year, in addition to being closely involved with local events marking the 50th anniversary of D-Day he will accompany over 100 members of the association to Caen in Normandy. His wife, Pearl, acts as his private secretary and is an associate member of the NVA and very proud to be so. She served in the ATS during the war.

David Preece was born on his family's Shropshire poultry farm, leaving school at about 15 because of the war. His father, a 1914-18 war veteran, returned to the Services. For 18 months David worked as a farm assistant for 2/6d a week, plus his keep!

When aged 16 he joined the Home Guard, having been refused admission as a regular soldier. However, when he was 17 he applied again, told the recruiting office he was 18 and became a private in the 70th Battalion Royal Warwickshire Regiment.

During his recruitment he had to undergo a medical examination. His consternation was considerable when the family doctor, who had delivered him into the world, appeared to examine him. "To his credit he said nothing," said the Major, "but I later learnt he telephoned my mother, who also told him to say nothing!" That was in March 1942. For training he went to Budbrook Barracks, Warwick, and recently attended a reunion of his old regiment.

In 1943 he moved to Exeter as an unpaid lance corporal. A colleague told him he had a date with an ATS girl in the Pay Corps, but as he had to go on duty asked David if he would stand in for him. That was how David met his wife!

He attended OCTU at Alton Towers, Staffordshire, and in January 1944 joined Number 3 Independent Machine Gun Company of the

127

Royal Northumberland Fusiliers in Norfolk. They were then training for D-Day On commissioning his age was officially corrected— to 19.

In each of the three armoured divisions preparing for the invasion there was a lorried infantry brigade. Number 3 Machine Gun Company, consisting of three platoons of Vickers plus one of heavy mortars, supported the 131 Lorried Infantry Brigade with the 7th Armoured Division.

Because he was the youngest officer in his unit he did not land on a Mulberry at Arromanches until D plus six. He took part in battles in Normandy including the Falaise Gap, outside Hambourg, where, in 1945, he was wounded, and finally rejoined his unit in Berlin.

He served with the Army of Occupation and to enable his wife— now a civilian— to join him in Germany deferred his demobilisation for a year. She was one of the first Service wives to go to Germany and, after this had been announced, was the recipient of several poison pen letters, on the lines of "Don't be unkind to the Germans by moving them out of their homes".

David was granted seven days leave in April 1945 in order to get married—and he arrived one day late because of stormy weather! The couple have two children—a son, a serving lieutenant colonel RA in London, and a daughter who lives in Cornwall.

David saw further service with the 1st Battalion Cheshire Regiment in Krefeld and finally, in 1969, left the Army after giving 27 years' service. In 1949 he had become a Regular officer, converting to the Royal Artillery.

The Veterans' Association, which meets monthly, is based at the Truro branch of the Royal British Legion. There are now over 100 members, who include a number in other parts of the country with wartime Cornish connections. Anyone who served in Normandy between D-Day and August 20 1944 is invited to join the association. I can put them in touch with the chairman.

These days David, a former sidesman at King Charles Parish Church, Falmouth, is a churchwarden there.

He emphasised that the anniversary of D-Day both in the UK and in France, would be in memory of fallen comrades. Those attending events will include parties of veterans from America (46 former members of the 29th Infantry Brigade) and Holland and the comprehensive programme should provide a fitting yet poignant reminder of those halcyon days half a century ago.

November 11, 1993

How the town remembered those who went to war

It was on Remembrance Sunday that an older Falmothian asked me if I still had my tribute fund gift and book presented by the town to all ex-service men and women. The answer was a decided affirmative, and proud I am of these items.

Many people in other parts of the country to whom I have shown these gifts have been envious and have said how much they wished their home towns had done something similar.

The Falmouth Tribute Fund booklet and the commemorative tankard

I particularly recall one meeting of the Tribute Fund Committee held in the council chamber. It was unusual because at the outset the chairman, Mr Bill Sargent, said he hoped the members of the press attending would take an active part in the meeting for they too were ex-servicemen and their opinions were needed.

129

This was the meeting when it was decided to present to each returning service person either a tankard, cigarette box or salver, each inscribed with the borough coat of arms, the date 1939-45 and the inscription "Falmouth's Token of Appreciation". Next of kin of those who lost their lives were also to receive gifts.

In addition, a record of the fund in book form in stiff covers again bearing the borough crest was also presented.

A preface to the book stated:

This Record has been prepared for all those who received tokens from the Falmouth Tribute Fund whether they be the next-of-kin of Falmothians who gave their lives on active service during the 1939-45 War or those who returned home to Falmouth after serving in His Majesty's Forces. A short history of the Fund may be of interest.

It was in November 1944, that the Falmouth Tribute Fund Committee launched an appeal for subscriptions in order to give personal recognition of services rendered by Falmothians in the Forces. The fund remained open until the end of 1945.

The dedication in 1945 of the sea-front shelter given to the town by the American forces in appreciation of the welcome they received in Falmouth

In October, 1945, a register of the names and addresses of potential recipients was compiled. It was decided at a public meeting held in July 1946, and attended by representatives of the Services, that the personal recognition of returning Service men and women should take the form of a choice, by the individual concerned, of one of three tokens of appreciation The articles were Cigarette Box, Tankard and Tray, each engraved with the Borough coat-of-arms and the words: "1939-45 Falmouth's Token of Appreciation".

The token of remembrance for the next-of-kin of the fallen should, it was later decided, be a Salver in sterling silver, with the name inscribed.

During 1947, six presentation ceremonies were held. On these several occasions 1,635 tokens were individually presented.

In February 1948, those who had not already received tokens stated the type of article they preferred and on the basis of the preferences so expressed the final batch of tokens was ordered.

Two further presentations took place privately, in June and July 1948, bringing the total number of tokens distributed to more than 1,800.

Section One of the book contains the names of men and women who gave their lives on active service during the 1939-45 War and whose next-of-kin received the token of remembrance provided by the fund.

The second section contains the names and addresses of men and women who served in the Forces during the 1939-45 war and received tokens on their return.

Mr. Sargent, who was licensee of the Wodehouse Inn on The Moor was a tireless worker for the fund. He later emigrated to Australia.

I am sure each of us who served during the war and the next of kin of those who lost their lives will always be grateful to the town for providing a permanent and detailed record and a gift worthy of display.

November 26, 1988

• Mayors of Falmouth during the Second World War years were as follows:- Messrs A.W. Reep (1937-1939); R.E. Gill, (1939/40); A.W. Reep (1941/42); E.E. Howard (1943/44/45).

Miracle Escape

Mr. Peter Harvey of Fish and Tackle in Webber Street, tells me that his late father, Albert, flew in Spitfires, being awarded the DSO. Albert, who came from Coverack, later flew Beaufighters and with his observer Bernard Wicksteed was the first to escape from one of these planes which ditched. They crashed in the sea at Mullion. A Heinkel which they had shot down had with its rear gun perforated the nose of the Beaufighter and as it sank the nose came off and the crew got out.

Mr. Albert Harvey later kept a tobacconist's shop at Market Strand Falmouth. Wicksteed wrote a book commemorating the escape and entitled "Father's Heinkel".

February 1992

Convoy Commodore once captain of *Ganges*

Last week the story of HMS *Ganges* was again revived with the review of a book bearing that title and written by a Carnmenellis resident who trained in that establishment.

There is another local link with that famous old training ship, for Hugh Hext Rogers OBE, later to become Rear Admiral, was Captain in charge at Harwich and Shotley *(HMS Ganges)* in 1933.

Mr Rogers, son of Mr Reginald Rogers, a solicitor at Falmouth, was born on October 27, 1883, at Carwinion, Mawnan Smith.

He was educated at *HMS Britannia* and had a distinguished naval career. In 1935 he was ADC to King George V and some years earlier was commander of the battle cruiser *HMS Renown* when she carried the then Prince of Wales on a world tour.

Outward-bound convoy No. 330 which left Liverpool on Monday, June 2 1941. Commodore Rogers notes: Uneventful till the convoy dispersed. Several ships sunk on the Canadian side of the Atlantic.

For many years Mr Rogers lived at Rock, near Wadebridge. When his mother died he moved back to Carwinion where he died in the late 1950s.

In September 1912 he married Agnes Channell, (who incidentally had her husband's portrait painted by Tuke). A grandson still lives in Mawnan Smith.

During the Second World War he was Commodore in charge of North Atlantic convoys, spending some 570 days at sea. An accomplished artist, he drew pictures of many of the ships he escorted.

March 10, 1990

American troops at Market Strand during exercise "Duck".

Yanks come back

June 9th 1990, 46 years after the 'D' day" landings, a party of Americans visited Falmouth to see again the port from which they had sailed on that historic occasion. For some members of the 41-strong party, which included wives, it was the first time they had seen Falmouth since 1944. The visit was organised by Mr. B.P. Allen, president of the USS LST 508 Association. His home is in Ohio. The party came to Falmouth from Plymouth and were entertained at a civic reception and received by the deputy mayor, Mrs. Olive White, in the absence of the Mayor, Cllr. Gordon Harrison.

From 12 to 1 pm they were the guests of Falmouth branch of the Royal Naval Association in the headquarters of Falmouth branch of the Royal British Legion. They later returned to Plymouth from where they set out to visit the 'D' day beaches. From October 1943 to July 1945 a US naval advanced amphibious base was in Falmouth. The King's hotel was their first home, repair work on vessels was carried out at the docks, a base was set up at the Beacon and various hotels housed US personnel including St. Michael's (a hospital), The Falmouth (finance section), Membly Hall and Greenbank. Their diary reads:

RETURN to NORMANDY

Forty-one former LSTers, including wives and families of 17 different LSTs, made a nostalgic return to Southern England and Normandy. The May 29 to June 10 tour was developed and expertly guided by Pat Combs of Combs Travel of Middletown, Ohio, Nigel Greenway of American Express and B.P. Allen, former CO of LST 508. List of those aboard are as follows with LST numbers: John and Mae Alleman, 508, Hummelstown, PA; B.P. and Ruth Allen, 508, Middletown, OH; Kenneth and Helen Arnold, 374, Northampton, MA; Ed Black, 57, Mt. Gilead, NC; Mrs. June Braddock, 508, Berlin, NJ; Lee and Kathy Braddock, 508, Albion, NJ; Mrs. Mavis Cooley, 508, LaCrosse, WI; Stuart, Joan and Jack Curtis, 537, Conneaut, OH; Henry and Dorothy DeJong, 508, Littleton, CO; Rudy Dosch, 345, Littleton, CO; Michael and Claire Ford, 374, Clark, NJ; George Henderson, 345, N. Andover, MA; Michael and Valerie Hutsell, 355, Massillon, OH; Ted and Helen Krajewski, 293, McKees Rock, PA; Grant and Marian Lee, 491 and 722, Enola, PA; Kenneth and Donna Mann, 266, Bloomington, IL; Frank and Vivian McAskill, 314/492 and 218/1026,

El Sobrante, CA; Grace Moore, 57, Charlotte, NC; Dean Peterson, 508, Phoenix, AZ; Ray Riggs, 508, Allentown, PA; Joseph Sardo, 290, Falls Church, VA; Joseph J. Schuchler, 508, Wilmington, DE; Robert L. Todd, 44, Arlington Heights, IL; Richard and Julia Vanderpool, 266, Dushore, PA; Richard and Jo Ellen Woolley, 316 and 500, San Diego, CA .

2 June - Morning tour to Falmouth where we were escorted to the Municipal Buildings by Mr. Eric Dawkins. Here the Council members and many other officials extended a warm and sincere welcome.

Mrs. Olive White, Deputy Mayor, presented group with a plaque of the Town of Falmouth; while we in turn presented gifts of our US LST Association consisting of the National Patch and medallion to them. Then a walk to the Royal Naval Association Club for refreshments and greetings, as guests of Cmdr. D.R. Thompson.

A late lunch was enjoyed at the Falmouth Hotel. Afterwards we returned to Plymouth.

June 9 1990

From the roar of aircraft engines to the peace of the Helford

Aircraft, rockets, cars, yachts and world travel. These are the components of the full life of an 81-year-old Mawnan resident with whom I recently spent a fascinating afternoon.

Roy Pearce, who admits he has led 'a very interesting life', was born in Bowden, Cheshire. He first visited Cornwall in the years 1927/28.

He secured a degree in engineering at Manchester University and was soon engaged in building massive steam railway engines for the Argentinian State Railways. To be inside the firebox of one of these monsters when someone hit it outside was an earsplitting experience!

This was the time of the great depression and soon afterwards he joined A V Roe and Company. Then, at the suggestion of his father, he decided to join the RAF in which, with his degree, he obtained a direct commission.

He learnt to fly in the Avro 504 - a single-engined bi-plane - and went on to a three-year operational tour with 111 Squadron in the London area. He recalled the occasion when, flying over fog there, his engine died. He came down through the cloud, fortunately to land in a field near the Kingston by-pass. It was imperative that he should specialise and he was posted to the RAF Training College at Henlow then the Imperial College in London.

It was at this time that he became involved with the Queen Bee - a radio controlled Tiger Moth - used for anti-aircraft gunnery practice.

His job was to travel around the country setting up the sites with catapults for launching the aircraft. Firing practice always took place over the sea and he worked at Watchett, Burrowhead Practice Camp in Wigtownshire, Manorbiere and Weybourne. The target float planes could be landed on the sea then retrieved by a launch .

In 1939 he set up a unit at Bude. 'We went into camp in May. We were in bell tents and it never stopped raining. I was CO, stores officer and medical officer. When my bedraggled men reported at each day's end, the medical officer would requisition rum from the stores officer and the CO would issue each man with a tot. We didn't have a single cold, though later when the men went into huts they suffered from colds and 'flu!'

It was in 1939 that Mr Pearce was married in Falmouth parish church by the Rector, the Rev O R M Roxby. Mrs Pearce, who had had links with Cornwall since she was 11 years of age, was the stepdaughter of Dr Sparks of Constantine who later moved into Falmouth. The couple now have two sons - Roger and Jeremy - and five grandchildren. One of Mr Pearce's proudest possessions is a gong in a wooden frame. The gong is the case of a 4.5 inch AA shell and the striker part of the joystick of a Queen Bee aircraft. It was presented to him on his marriage by the Bude detachment. Mr and Mrs Pearce had a home at this time at the corner of Woodlane. Falmouth.

When war broke out he was posted to the Ministry of Aircraft production and he was also a member of the technical branch of the RAF. He was in charge of the receiving end of the American aircraft on loan under the Lend-Lease plan. He met many famous pilots and commuted between the UK and USA on liaison work, getting to know the Lockheed Bell company. Many of the bigger aircraft were flown over, but he had direct responsibility for those which came by sea and which had to be constructed here. He himself flew many types of aircraft, admitting to a preference for the Mosquito and Mustang. He has also flown Vampire and Meteor Jets.

There was a growing involvement with Australia at this time and soon he was posted to that continent where he met Jimmy Martin of Martin Baker and Company. He was pursuaded to sit in an early ejector seat which was then fired. He still suffers today as a result of the sudden jar to his spine. Later models were modified.

Again, Down Under, he was engaged in liaison work with the government and industry and also worked closely with the Australian Air Force.

He went on a 'stepping stones' flight to New Guinea and Borneo and remembered at one station seeing a film shown on a sheet strung between trees. While he was watching, an Australian tapped him on the shoulder and told him to look in the trees behind. All around were little men - unarmed Japanese - taking a look. At this time the Allies had leap-frogged forward, leaving isolated pockets of the enemy.

Then Mr Churchill sent General Sir John Evett to oversee the development of a long-range rocket in South Australia. Mr Pearce worked with the RAAF to survey the site of a theoretical centre for a rocket range. He flew 1,100 miles with an Australian crew to the Northern Territory, tracing a likely flight path for rockets. All the way vertical pictures were taken of the terrain over which they passed and he remembered that when attempting to land for fuel a line of kangaroos had blocked the runway!

Prior to this Mr Pearce had piloted a B24 Liberator bomber from America across the Pacific, via Honolulu to Australia.

The rocket site, which was set up later and which was to become famous, was at Woomera.

Returning to the UK, Mr Pearce spent another five or six years with the RAF, retiring in 1952.

He was approached by Rolls Royce in connection with a plan to build big engines for the Blue Streak rocket. These were American engines being constructed under licence. He had to organise a testing area near Carlisle, in the Fells of Cumbria, and in 1958 returned to Woomera. Later the Blue Streak programme was cancelled and in 1965 Mr Pearce joined the Rover company.

He was managing director of a firm which produced Rover gas turbines used in projects which included portable fire pumps for the Royal Navy, marine propulsion and a radio controlled target drone. He demonstrated a Rover turbo car, later driven by Graham Hill, but this vehicle developed technical problems and was dropped. In 1967 he left Rover.

Mr and Mrs Pearce came back to Cornwall, where they owned Polwhaveral Cottage and took over the boatyard at Ponsharden, Falmouth, which they named Ponsharden Marine Services. They ran this for 20 years. Two and a half years ago they transferred to their present home which has been built as an annexe to a son's house.

'Since we were married, and thanks to Service life, we have moved 52 times,' laughed Mrs Pearce, 'We have lived in caravans, Service quarters and huts.'

There is another facet of Mr Pearce's life - one with which he has had a constant romance - that of yachting. He and his brother started sailing in 1934/35 and became friends with the designer of the famous Kival yachts. They bought a barge in Birkenhead, named her Makrojak ('my first wife,' jokes Mr Pearce) and converted her into a 42ft Bermudan cutter, sailing her in July 1939 from Liverpool to the Helford river.

Both Mr Pearce and his son Jeremy have a love for working on and rebuilding wooden boats. He told me he had sailed many types of yachts but had never owned one until now - he and his son own the yacht Saromo, built by Burt of Falmouth in the 1940s. Mr Pearce has rigged her with a spritsail which he has designed and which is used in Thames barges. Now this much-travelled man contentedly sits in his sitting room, overlooking a peaceful creek off the Helford river where his yacht is laid up for the winter - the direct antithesis to the roar of aircraft or rocket engines and a whole world away from America and Australia.

December 14, 1991

Falmouth and the Victoria Cross awards

During the Second World War, 22 VCs were earned by naval personnel. One of these was Able Seaman William Alfred Savage from Smethwick, Birmingham, who lost his life in the St. Nazaire raid.

Mr. Savage, who is buried in Falmouth cemetery, died as he manned a pom pom gun during the operation designed to cripple the only dry dock in Western Europe capable of berthing the German battleship *Tirpitz*.

On June 28 this year the Victoria Cross awarded to Able Seaman Savage was auctioned at Sotheby's in London.

At this time I was in contact with Mr. Brad Smith of Southsea who is particularly interested in the history of the award which is the highest this country can give for valour in war. He undertook to give me details of links between Falmouth and the Victoria Cross and writes:

"William Savage is one of three holders of the Victoria Cross to be connected with Falmouth. The other two were born in Falmouth but lie buried elsewhere. The town has connections with four other Victoria Cross holders and they were in the same action with Savage at the raid on St. Nazaire (Operation Chariot) commemorated on Falmouth's harbour front by a memorial to the raid.

"There is a Savage Close named after him in the former Navy Married Quarters estate in Rowner, Gosport, Hampshire.

"The first of the three was born William Odgers, the son of a Falmouth Packet man who was born in Falmouth in 1833, although there is some doubt as to the year if the inscription on his headstone is correct. He won his Victoria Cross in New Zealand March 28 1860 while serving with HMS Niger and was gazetted with the Medal a few months later. It would appear that he did not live in Falmouth for long as all other traces of him refer to Saltash, also in Cornwall.

"William Odgers was a leading seaman in the Royal Navy when he won the award and went on to become a quartermaster and later a Boatman with the Coastguard. He retired through ill health and settled in Saltash where he was landlord of a public house there called 'the Union Inn'. It still stands there today and although the name has been changed to 'The Union' the original name can still be seen on the inn's side looking down from the Saltash bridge.

"He married twice and never fully recovered from ill health and died at the age of 40 at the Union Inn on December 20, 1873, and lies buried in the churchyard of St. Stephen's-by-Saltash in an unmarked grave. The headstone is still there but was removed from its original position when the graveyard section was tidied up. The inscription on his headstone reads as follows. 'Sacred to the memory Anne Odgers (late of Saltash) wife of William Odgers, who departed this life 28th Feb. 1865 aged 35 years. Also George Jenkins (late Saltash) who departed this life 1st July 1859 aged 21 years. Also William Odgers V.C. who departed this life 20th Dec 1873 aged 40 years. His end was peace.'

"The third Victoria Cross was awarded to another Falmouth-born man in the town April 11, 1906. He was James Power Carne who won the Victoria Cross in Korea April 22/23, 1951 in the Imjin area. He was serving as a Lieutenant Colonel in command of the 1st Battalion, the Gloucestershire Regiment when he won his award. He carved a cross made of stone for prison camp services and it is now preserved in Gloucester Cathedral. He went on to become Deputy Lieutenant for the County of Gloucestershire and in addition to his V.C. he was awarded the DSO and received the DSC from the United States. His medals were presented to the Glosters Regimental Museum by his widow in 1986 (Mrs. Jean Carne).

"His final rank in the Army was that of Colonel and he died at Cheltenham on April 19, 1986, aged 80 years. The funeral service took place at Cranham Church on Friday April 25, 1986, and following cremation at Cheltenham his ashes were laid to rest in Cranham Churchyard on the western boundary. The spot is marked with a simple stone tablet and there is a memorial plaque in the church."

I have discovered yet another holder of the Victoria Cross who had links with Falmouth. He was Field Marshal Sir George Stuart White and details of the life of this distinguished soldier are as follows:

"Was born July 6, 1835, and married Amy, daughter of the Ven. Archdeacon Baly, curate-in-charge at Falmouth 1870, and a granddaughter of the Rev. William John Coope, Rector of Falmouth 1838-70. Sir George entered the Army in 1853, served in Indian Mutiny; Afghan War 1878-80; March from Kabul to Kandahar; decorated with Victoria Cross for conspicuous bravery during the action at Charaziab, October 1879, and at Kandahar 1880; Nile expedition 1884-85; Commander Brigade in Burma 1885-86; conducted expedition into Zhob; Commander-in-Chief of the Force in India 1893-98; defended Ladysmith from November 2, 1899 to March 1, 1900."

September 29, 1990

Captured by the Nazis

Bert Hutson of Oakfield Road, Falmouth, who was a member of the crew of the *SS British Commander*, sunk by an enemy raider in August 1940, and who was prisoner-of-war number 91401 in the Milag Nord prison camp at Westertinke near Bremen, has given me this dramatic account of his experiences then.

'We sailed from England on July 16 1940. Nearly six weeks later, at 4.15am on the morning of August 27, an enemy raider intercepted us. We were shelled and torpedoed without warning, but all hands were saved with no casualties. The German raider picked us up and imprisoned us in the forward section 'tween decks.

'For three weeks we lived on black bread, sausage and potatoes, with one mug of coffee per man. We were allowed on deck for an hour each day. When the raider went into action against merchantmen, mostly unarmed, everyone was battened down. With her 5" and 6" guns blazing away the noise was terrific and were were very glad when the battle finished. After a while the hatches would be opened and the survivors, many of whom were badly wounded, were brought down to live with us.

'On September 20 we were transferred to a Norwegian prison ship which brought us to Bordeaux after nine and a half weeks dodging about the Southern Ocean. We lay alongside in Bordeaux for three weeks while for two nights following the RAF bombed shipping and docks. Luckily, we did not get hit.

'Two days after we were on our way to Draney civil internee prison camp, near Paris. We spent five hungry months there and during that time received only one Red Cross food parcel. Tobacco, like food, was very scarce, but in spite of all that everyone was cheerful and in good spirits, while most of us indulged in football, table tennis and sundry other games. New arrivals, all merchant seamen, from all parts of the globe, soon filled our camp.

'In April the German high command ordered us to leave for the "Fatherland". The march through the streets of Le Bourget to the station we thoroughly enjoyed.

'On leaving camp someone produced a cornet, another a guitar, while others played their mouth organs the rest of us (700 men) singing, the most popular song being "Sons of the Sea". This was sung with real feeling as we tramped along with Jerry guards on either side, some smiling sarcastically, others trying to stop us singing, but nothing could stop us then, only a bullet!

The French population played up to us magnificently by lining the streets and cheering us on with cries of "Long live France and England". Young French women were in the majority, threw us loaves of white bread and biscuits, defying the guards who threatened to shoot if they did not stop. People waved from windows and doors, most of them with tears running down their faces, a sight which brought a lump to our throats. But this only made us sing more heartily than ever as we waved back to our allies.

By the time we reached the station the guards had lost their tempers and unceremoniously bundled us into cattle trucks.

'We were packed 40 to a truck with loose straw to lie on. Black bread and sausage were our rations for 24 hours, six men to a loaf. This uncomfortable train journey came to and end after three days and we were now in Germany, most of us for the first time.

The reception given to us by the German people was entirely different from that of the French. The German fraus and frauleins spat at us, jeered and cursed, calling us "English pigs and swines".

Naturally we resented this and replied back in no uncertain terms, as only true British seamen can.

July 17, 1993

Attempt to solve a wartime mystery

For a year, M. Albert Lecocq of 1, Rue Pierre Marquis, 27250 Rugles, in Normandy, has been attempting to solve the mystery of two Lancaster bombers which crashed in Rugles and Cheronvilliers, a small community some three kilometres from Rugles on the nights of August 15 and 16, 1943.

His researches have revealed a possible Falmouth area link with a member of one of the aircraft crews and he has written to Falmouth's mayor seeking information.

I have agreed to publish the request with the hope that a reader may be able to help. Mr. Lecocq writes:

"The bomber which was shot down in Rugles had exploded with its load of bombs, on the way to raid Milan (Italy). Only the pilot was able to escape by parachute.

Four members of the crew were buried in the cemetery of our village. As for the two other airmen their bodies have never been found for they were destroyed by the explosion of the bombs. They were: Flight Officer Tom Downing (bomb aimer) and C. Andy Angwin, (wireless operator).

"Through the survivor, Pilot Victor Matthews, I have learned that the mother of Andy Angwin whom he visited on his return to England, was living in the centre of London but he could not remember the name of the street.

"Mrs. Elizabelh Lucas Harrison, secretary of the Royal Air Forces Escaping Society at 206 Brompton Road, in London, who I have asked if she could help me, tried to locate the relatives of Andy Angwin.

"She found only one family in London which bears the same family name, but has no knowledge of the airman.

"Mrs. Lucas Harrison told me she had found that the family name "Angwin" originated from Cornwall and that several persons in your town bear this family name. I wonder if they are related to Andy Angwin?

"On September 8 and 9, the municipalities of Rugles and Cheronvilliers welcome officially at a reception the two survivors of these two crashes as well as the families of the lost victims I had been able to locate.

October 13, 1990

A tragic accident

Mr Norman C. Bishop of Tremorvah, Swanpool Road, Falmouth writes

"Your excellent article in the Leader regarding "Q" ships certainly stirred up memories.

I remember an unfortunate accident which happened in the *Mary B. Mitchell.*

"Following the First World War she was moored alongside the Prince of Wales Pier and opened up to the public. Crew members showed patrons around the ship describing various components used during the war. One crew member, explaining one of the guns was unaware it was loaded. He pulled the trigger and fired a live shell.

"One lady—a Miss Vincent who was in line opposite the gun muzzle was hit and had to have her damaged leg amputated.

"As in those days artificial limbs were unheard of she walked with a crutch for the rest of her life. She had been employed as shop assistant in Lake's Falmouth Packet shop and printing works at the bottom of the High Street (now Menzies).

"After her accident, although she was semi-mobile, Ivan Lake, one of the Falmouth Packet proprietors kindly re-employed her as shop assistant.

"Apart from this unfortunate accident the *Mary B, Mitchell* most certainly had a wonderful war record."

July 14, 1990

Russian Convoy memories

One of the most enjoyable weekly social gatherings in Penryn is that of the Monday Saracen Lunch Club at the Temperance Hall. There, over 40 people, all of whom have long-established links with the old town, meet for a first-class meal and to reminisce about bygone days.

The club was started three years ago by Gloria Seviour of Carrick Council's home help department. Present chairman is Harold Hazzard, with Plymothian Roy Blake secretary and treasurer.

Roy is a member of the local branch of the Royal Naval Association, Penryn Club and the South West Russian Convoy Club, which incorporates Royal and Merchant Navy personnel and has some 50-60 active members, meeting regularly at Devonport. He is also a sidesman at St Gluvias church.

He came to Penryn in 1955. after he was a chief electrician. He has also worked at Falmouth docks. He joined the RN as a boy seaman in 1934, going to *HMS Ganges* at Shotley. He went on *HMS Royal Sovereign* then to the Mediterranean serving on *HMS Delhi*, a cruiser. 'Dusty' Millar, a RNA member who died recently, was also a boy seaman with Roy. The couple next met many years later on a parade in Falmouth when Dusty was standard bearer for the Falmouth branch of the British Legion.

Prior to her sinking in Scapa Flow, Roy served in the battleship *HMS Royal Oak*, then was a crew member of *HMS Rodney* when war was declared. He proceeded to Mombasa (Freetown) where he joined *HMS Albatross*, a former New Zealand seaplane carrier.

He later saw service in *HMS Caesar*, a member of the VIth destroyer flotilla. He was two years and nine months on board *Albatross* and two-and-a-half years with *Caesar*. While with *Caesar* he made several trips to Russia encountering extreme cold and violent weather. He finally left the Navy in 1949, joined the RNR in 1950 was recalled that year because of the Korean War. He was posted to Hong Kong and *HMS Consort*, a destroyer, eventually leaving the service in 1955.

Thereafter, he worked in the electrical department at Falmouth docks. In 1960 Ray's family suffered a great tragedy when his youngest son, then aged 16 and having just started an apprenticeship at the docks, was drowned at Trefusis. An elder son, Eric, is now the headmaster of Steps Cross School, Torquay. Roy's wife died five years ago.

Roy enjoys the comradeship of his fellow ex-servicemen and likes nothing better than serving Penryn's older citizens—a task which, to judge by some of their comments, they greatly appreciate.

March 20, 1993

Prior to embarkation US troups taking part in exerciuse "Duck" are given a hot meal, cigarettes,candy and "short beef". Phot was probably taken near The Moor.

Zeppelin raids

One of our best known senior citizens — Mrs Dorothy Congdon, of Langholme, Arwenack Avenue, tells me that when she recently returned trom a two weeks' holiday in Southampton she found the 'Leader' for week ending May 20 referring to war days in Falmouth. She tells me: "We in Cornwall knew nothing much about the First World War; not in Flushing, anyhow. I must have been about 16 years of age and was staying in Devoran. My cousins took me to Baldhu where there was a concert and I learnt a song there about the Kaiser, which we sang all the way back (walking):

'Oh Mr Kaiser what are you going to do?
Don't forget you have to fight the Red, the White, the Blue
Mind what you're about, old chap and don't you be too rash
We'll wipe you out of the Union Jack
And we'll cut off your big moustache.'

"Little did I know then that when I was 18 years of age I was going to Maidstone to live with a great aunt, a retired lady's maid, who had been left a house. She wrote to my mother: You have a lot of daughters, so send me one to live with me.' There was no news on TV or the wireless to tell us what it was like there — not in Flushing anyhow! So my mother said to me, 'You go!' Well, I travelled to London on my own. My great aunt met me in Paddington Station.

"Her first words were: 'What a little small thing. Didn't your mother have anyone bigger than you to send?' That was enough to make me wonder why I had left home. We went by horse and cabs to another station.

"Well, I had one year of that awful time. The Zeppelins, with their fire bombs, came over Maidstone more often than over Chatham. We had no warnings in those days. We just heard them come over the house. One night it was terrible. I was at a church service and when we were walking home we were falling over each other.

"Then in the night, the corner of my room lit up and I heard a voice telling me it was alright. Some people may say this was a mirage, but being a Christian I knew our Lord was with me.

"I came home a wreck and those experiences have lived with me ever since. Now I must sit in the back of the hall wherever I go. If I can't hear, people suggest I come to the front, but I can't explain all this to them. In the last war we were living at Roscrow and a large piece of shrapnel hit my face.

"Incidentally, my aunt eventually came to Cornwall, to Mawgan near Helston, where she lived with a niece. The toilet was at the top of the garden. She fell and broke her hip. Medical science was not so advanced in those days and at 60-odd she passed away. It was a sad ending.

June 17, 1989

InDecember 1943 a LCT loaded with vehicles leaves the old submarine pier during exercise "Duck".

Runners were sent on secret sea missions

Information about the war years in this area continues to filter out, often in the most unexpected places. Chatting recently in Constantine with Ronnie Rashleigh, a former shipwright and employee of Falmouth Boat Construction, he told me about the 'ball bearing runners'. These were very fast, unarmed craft, each powered by three diesels and painted a mauve colour. This was camouflage, enabling the craft to blend into the colour of the cliffs near where they anchored. He remembers seeing three at Coastlines badly shot up. So highly secret were they that they were covered with tarpaulins.

Gay Viking

Many years later, from a shipwright (Clive Temperten, now of Mawgan), he learned the half dozen or so of these vessels were known as Grey Wolves. Each bore a name with the first word *Gay*. Mr Temperten had worked on *Gay Viking*. The craft were used to dash across the North Sea to obtain ball bearings.

Because Sweden was a neutral country they were unarmed. There, German crews (on a similar mission) and the British might be drinking in the same bar! But when the vessels made the return journey they had to run the gauntlet of air attacks.

Mr Rashleigh said he understood the boats were based in Immingham. At the time he saw them at Boyers Cellars George Nicholls was the boat construction foreman.

It is understood that a bale of calico (needed to effect repairs and extremely rare in wartime) had been delivered at the express order of Winston Churchill.

Mr Rashleigh further mentioned Lord Runciman's fine three masted, grey painted yacht, *Sunbeam*, which was a Royal Naval HQ ship moored in the Helford River during the war.

He remembered how shortly before D-Day the bus taking them to work left Constantine at 5am and drove via Helston, near Hayle, Camborne and Sithney to get to Falmouth! On the morning after the Swanvale oil tanks were bombed the roads at recreation ground corner were covered with fire hoses with protective coverings, over which the bus bumped.

June 19, 1993

More on the MGBs

Recent revelations by Ronnie Rashleigh of Constantine about the wartime 'Runners' - fast vessels used to bring ball bearings from Sweden - has brought the following from Mr T Anderson of Mongleath Avenue, Falmouth .

'There were eight of those craft originally designed as gunboats (MGBs) in 1942. They were MGBs 502-509, but only 502, 503 and 509 were completed as gunboats - the other five were completed as blockade runners and carried a 45 ton cargo in that capacity.

'MGB 504 renamed as *Hopewell*; MGB 505 *Nonsuch*; MGB 506 *Gay Viking* (lost 1944) MGB 507 *Gay Corsair*: MGB 508 *Masteil Standfast* (lost 1943); MGBs 504, 505 and 506 built at Gosport and 507 and 508 at Northam by Camper and Nicholson .'

July 17, 1993

Sir George and the runners

Recent stories about the ball bearing runners going to and from this country and Sweden, have aroused much interest.

From Mr G E Sharpe of 15 Higher Market Street, Penryn, I have received the following:

Some years ago I worked for a gentleman in Essex, Sir George Binney, although at the time of the runners he was just George Binney.

On the outbreak of war George was a purchasing agent for high quality bearings, obtained from Sweden, an important commodity in wartime. When Norway and Denmark were invaded by Germany some ships took refuge in Swedish ports. These were, on the instructions of George, loaded with bearings, which he intended to be delivered to England.

However, the Gestapo were present, as civilians, and they took the matter to the Swedish courts, claiming the ships belonged to Germany as spoils of war.

Luckily, the courts disagreed, pointing out that the ships were already under charter to George Binney, and that while under charter they were his property.

It was one thing beating the Germans in court, but quite another to get the ships to England as German forces were waiting. Five ships set sail and as I remember only one arrived in the UK.

It was then Sir George's idea, along with Sir Peter Thornycroft, that they should design very high speed low draft vessels that could cross straight over the heavily mined areas around the coasts of Denmark and Sweden, get in and out fast. This they did, and very successfully.

They were, of course, attacked and some very badly damaged. Peter Thornycroft was, I understand, severely wounded during one of these runs.

Both were knighted for their efforts.

Sir George wrote a book about his exploits. He died some years ago in Jersey.

July 24, 1993

Torpedoed off The Lizard

Throughout August and early September Falmouth Art Gallery presented an exhibition of watercolours entitled 'The Inheritance of the Hart Family'.

This remarkable family, who made Cornwall and, in particular, The Lizard and the Falmouth area the focus of their art, had as its figurehead and father Thomas Hart, who was born at Crowan in 1830.

In 1862 he married a Penzance woman and had 12 children, of whom six were credited as artists.

This exhibition, which was the first showing of works by the Harts in Cornwall since they were alive, contained over 50 watercolours, several oil portraits, photographs, sketchbooks and other memorabilia.

Much help in staging the show was given by Mrs J Hart of Parc an Castle on The Lizard.

In her lovely home, so close to The Lizard lighthouse, and with a vast panorama of sea spread below us, we talked of Falmouth, where Mrs Hart was born.

Her parents lived for a short time in a private hotel or boarding house, now a government office, nearly opposite the entrance to the docks, and it was there that she was born.

At Easter 1939 she was married at Landewednack and the couple settled at The Lizard. Her husband had been born in New Zealand, to which her father-in-law had emigrated, returning to the UK just before the Great War.

He took a job with the Falmouth Electric Light Company and he and his wife lived in Church Street in the flat over what is now the SWEB shop.

Mrs Hart's father-in-law was an engineer at the docks in the days of Cox and Company.

Mrs Hart came to Parc an Castle in 1916 and now has the distinction of being the person who has lived the longest in one house in The Lizard.

Inevitably our conversation turned to the war years and memories of the Second World war, with amazing reminiscences from the Great War days.

Mr Hart's work with the electricity company was classified as a reserved occupation. He had to do fire watching and a requirement was that he manned a telephone there every night.

"Most people left Church Street at night and there were very few of us left there. It was rumoured there were no hydrants in the main street and we always wondered how we should cope if incendiaries were dropped," she told me.

She recalled that the day a mine exploded in the inner harbour her husband had watched the column of water rise with a barge, in which men had been working, on the top.

She described the days around the Dunkirk evacuation as "a dismal time". The bay was full of ships of all sizes including three or four big Dutch liners in their peacetime colours and flying house flags which she recognised, having watched them passing The Lizard on many occasions. Later they were all painted a camouflage grey and could not be so easily identified.

Just after D-Day Mrs Hart visited her mother at Parc-an-Castle. From there she watched an unescorted battle cruiser (she thinks it was *HMS Rodney*) steaming past at speed. Her mother told her she had never seen so many ships passing The Lizard.

Another war memory was of watching the old destroyer *HMS Campbeltown* gliding out of Falmouth harbour. Long after they realised she had been setting out for St Nazaire and that epic raid. Years later Capt Beattie VC, her commander, was the honorary secretary of The Lizard lifeboat.

And then as Mrs Hart and I gazed down on seas breaking over rocks off The Lizard, came the Great War memory.

"From this house in 1917 I watched a ship being torpedoed off here. At that time the German U-boats were very active in these waters. A column of water rose alongside the ship which heeled over. It could have been the *Beluchia* which sank off Church Cove and is now a fishlng mark."

Lord Sempill had had a house near Parc an Castle many years later, and he had entertained a German ex-submariner who knew the coast intimately.

Mrs Hart's husband died in 1954. There is a daughter, Elizabeth, who keeps the Wave Crest cafe overlooking the most southerly point at The Lizard.

Again and again the conversation returned to war days. Mrs Hart reminisced that the night the Dutchmen arrived in Falmouth after Holland had fallen, she and her husband went to the Town Quay. "The number of girls who found a Dutchman for the evening was wonderful."

In 1941 when a stick of bombs fell on the waterfront, the downstairs windows of their flat were blown out.

After two world wars Parc-an-Castle, a solid granite house, stands foursquare facing the worst weather to come in from the sea, while inside Mrs Hart relives virtual frontline memories spanning over 70 packed vears.

October 14, 1993

Local wartime craft

Recent articles about Falmouth Boat Construction and the wartime craft built by this firm have caused much interest. The following letters have been received.

Mr F R Axford, of Comfort Road, Mylor, writes:

'I served in ML 491. We were first stationed at Dartmouth (as SO of the 7th Flotilla) from 1942-43, then the flotilla was dispersed and 491 moved to Falmouth. The boats were now being fitted with navigational gear, including echo sounders, I believe to enable them to lead the groups of assault ships to the beaches of Normandy. We took part in the rehearsals and once had General Omar Bradley on board for a close-up inspection of the action, bombardments of Slapton Sands etc. However, I left the boat before D-Day being surplus to requirements as we were no longer senior officer of a flotilla. I have met some of the crew since and happy to say that the boat and crew survived the war. We never went to the training base in Scotland, Fort William, as we were already an experienced crew, previously on ML 270, which was scuttled on the return trip from the St Nazaire raid. Speaking of which, when the survivors of that raid returned to St Nazaire last April we saw a monument to those who had lost their lives in the Lancastria. This, I believe, was fairly recent as I did not see it in 1982.

'Which reminds me that there is another monument in Falmouth, as well as Kimberley Park, and that is in the cemetery and was erected by the Missions to Seamen.

'Incidentally, when ML 491 was based in Falmouth (or was it Penryn, being at Coast Lines Jetty?) the crew once took part in a boat (gig??) race against a crew of workers from the yard. Needless to say we lost, for they knew the river better than us.'

Then, from Mr T George of Penryn, came the following:

'In further reference to details previously published, concerning craft built by the Boat Construction Company at Falmouth in World War Two, I enclose (below) details of those same craft, with the addition of dates when it is believed that they were completed and with details of their end or removal from the Royal Navy.

'I am in no way an authority in this matter. The information I have is generally from 'accepted sources'; in other words, just hearsay.

'The reader last mentioned on the subject suggested that MTB 675 (rather than 678) and 1006 (rather than 5006) ought to be included. Maybe, but MTB 675 was constructed in Argyllshire and, to my knowledge, MTB/MGB numbers never reached four digits; I think they were to have got into the 900 range but never did. HDML numbers were always in four digits and using 1006 as such a craft that was built in Littlehampton.

'During 1946, or thereabouts, two MTBs were loaned to Falmouth Sea Cadet Corps - these were MTB 610 and 617. The first went to Weymouth SCC in 1950 and 617 was sold in 1953. One of these was renamed Trefusis while at Falmouth and further information on that may be worthy of inclusion in your column.

'Towards the end of World War Two the newer craft were given numbers with four digits and certainly in mid-1949 this happened with the re-designation of FPB (fast patrol boat) taking over the more familiar ML, MTB, MGB prefix letters.'

Boat Construction Company,
Falmouth, Fairmile B Type ML,
Fairmile D Type MGB/MTB

ML 137 (completed 11/1940) occurs up for disposal 10/1945; ML 164 (1211940), on loan service with Royal Netherlands Navy, sold 1946; ML 187 (2/1941), sold at Singapore (6/1947): ML 226 (4/1941), occurs up for disposal at Freetown 1945; ML 261 (6/1941), occurs up for disposal at Freetown 1945; ML 271(7/1941), became V102 in French Navy 1944; ML 336 (9/1941),to Italian Navy 1945; ML 446 (11/1941), lost at St Nazaire 1942; ML 471 (4/1942), to Italian Navy 1946, ML491(511942), renumbered ML 2491 1949, sold 1961, MGB 635 (11/1942), damaged during 1944 and sunk as target off Malta 7/1945; MGB 650 (1/1943), to RAF 1945 as long range rescue craft LRRC 020; MGB 659 (5/1943), lost 1/46 on passage Malta-Alexandria- MGB 678 (7/1943) to RAF 1945 as LRRC 026; MTB 690 (9/1943), lost by collision with wreck in North Sea; MTB 707 (11/1943); lost by collision with *L'Escarmouche*, north of Ireland; MTB 725 (3/1944), to Sea Cadet Corps Pwllheli in 1945 and sold 9/1951; MTB 753 (7/1944), to SCC Bermondsey in 1945, sold 10/1956; MTB 767 (12/1944), occurs up for disposal (1/1947); MTB 790 (7/1945), 1949 becomes FP8 5003 until sold 1953; MTB 5006 (8/1945), to RAF 8/1945 as LRRC 004, until later returned to Admiralty.

NB About the middle of 1949 all MTB/MGB Coastal Force craft were renumbered and known as Fast Patrol Boats.

January 9, 1993

How the Q9 sank four U boats

Recent references to the famous 'Q' ship *Mary B Mitchell* or *MBM* as she was known in Great War days would seem to have stirred memories for a number of people.

Retired Falmouth dentist Gordon Mann, who formerly practised in Market street, told me that when living as a young boy in Ayrshire, his next door neighbour was Captain John Laurie, famous skipper of the *Mary B. Mitchell.*

Mr. Mann said that he and Captain Laurie's two sons frequently sat wide eyed and fascinated as his father (who had served in the Army) and Captain Laurie swapped stories about their First World War exploits.

He believed the Captain had been awarded the DSO and DSC bar. During the Second World War he had sailed on the dangerous Murmask run and had been awarded the "Order of the Red Banner" by the Russians. Later he went on Atlantic convoys, his ship was torpedoed and he lost his life. "He was a real sea dog and one of the finest characters I have ever known" said Mr. Mann. "I am sure his boys and I were told stories of his experiences that they had never previously heard."

Yet Mr. Mann himself is no ordinary character. He first came to Falmouth in 1948, subsequently became a member then President of Falmouth Rotary Club and honorary member of the Penryn Club and is a past District Governor. Now for six seasons under the auspices of Rotary International he has been giving his services to people in the Philippines, Hong Kong , in the Amazon area and the Bolivean jungle. Later this year he will be going to the Far East again. He said he had spent much time with the Vietnamese boat people for whom he had a great affection.   Here are extracts from the log of the *Q9, HMS Mary B Mitchell*, compiled originally by J. Manley, mate:-

"It was on April 10 1916 that the good old *Mary B.* was commandeered by the Government at Swansea and taken to Falmouth to be fitted out for special service, becoming one of the Mystery Ships destined with similar vessels to take such a great part in combatting the German submarine menace which at this time and particularly 12 months later looked like throttling the life out of our country. So the *Mary B. Mitchell*, an innocent coasting schooner was transformed into the *Q9.*

"Manned by a volunteer crew of Naval Reserve Men principally recruited from the Mercantile Marine and fishermen, she set out upon her first six weeks' cruise in the three Channels, English, St. Georges and Bristol and to the Westward of the Scilly Isles but no luck came our way on that or any subsequent cruises until December 2, then our chance came.

"It was 10 am in the English Channel when about 15 miles South of the Wolf Lighthouse the lookout aloft reported a submarine three points off the starboard bow towing two lifeboats. Our Commander ordered the guns' crews to stand by for action. At this time we were armed with one 12 Pounder, two 6 Pounders and a Maxim gun and were without auxiliary propelling power.

"We allowed the submarine to approach to within 100 yards. Fritz hoisted signals and shouted through his megaphone to abandon ship immediately as he was about to sink us. Orders were given for five hands to remain on deck to back the yards and heave to, while the remainder of the ship's company were concealed under the hatchways in readiness for action.

"The action bell rings, the hatches fall off, the ship's sides fall away and we get in four direct hits on *U 26*. A heavy explosion occurred and the *U 26* blew up disappearing as she took her last dive bow first.

"The second enemy submarine with whom the *U 26* was working came to the surface and fired a torpedo across our stern, we not being able to manoeuvre with only plain sail. Fritz disappeared and we got the two lifeboats alongside which we found contained a crew of 22 men from a torpedoed Norwegian steamer. The crew gave us a rousing cheer and said that ours was a funny cargo ship. They were taken on board a trawler and landed at Penzance.

"We then made for the Scilly Isles—St. Mary's, where we again disguised our rig.

"Several abortive cruises followed and in the meantime our armament was increased by one 4 inch, one 12 pounder, three 6 pounders, two Lewis guns and hand grenades. We also had two powerful motors.

"It was not until June 1917 that we again came into contact with the enemy 200 miles S.W. of The Lizard. We had been on patrol 12 days and were making our passage home to our base when the lookout reported a ship's lifeboat under sail two points abaft our starboard beam. This, as we thought, turned out to be a German submarine with sails set as a decoy. A few minutes later he opened up rapid fire at a range of about three miles but his aim was erratic. Closing in on our starboard side he gave us three rounds across our bow. The ship was again abandoned, by our "panic crew" of seven men. Fritz closed in and took shots at our main mast and yards but failed and, coming to the conclusion that we were unarmed, he submerged and reappeared within 50 yards on our port side.

"Action orders were given and our after gun got in a direct hit under the conning tower at point blank range while we swept the submarine crew from her deck with our Lewis gun fire. A moment later our 12 pounders got in several hits on her hold. She then blew up and disappeared. This was a glorious scrap. Getting our panic crew onboard again we sailed for home, but an hour later another submarine was reported on the port bow. They steamed full speed for us and again our "panic crew" took to the boat. Fritz sent along a lot of hot stuff trying to hit our mast and yard over the side, but he was very artful and was closing with us. In the meantime all we could do was to lie concealed at the guns and await chances. Fritz getting tired of waiting gradually crept closer and when the submarine was within 200 yards from us on our port bow, we opened fire on him, and poured 30 rounds into the sub getting 11 direct hits. She rolled over and disappeared in a cloud of smoke.

"We got our "panic party" onboard again and got on our course for Ushant, 200 miles E.S.E. quite satisfied with ourselves. At 8 pm we sighted another sub, two miles astern but she did not trouble us. We arrived the following day at our base after an exciting patrol which will always live in our memories. We logged 270 miles for the days' run with strong Westerly Wind.

"The next occasion on which we came in contact with the enemy was August 16, 1917, 23 miles S.E. of Start Point. A submarine was reported by wireless 12 miles south of Start Point, so we proceeded to look for another scrap. At about 1.15 pm a sub was reported when all hands were at dinner. This submarine put a shot across our bow and the "panic party" got ready to abandon ship. Fritz started shelling us at 2,000 yards but without effect. After an hour the sub, one of the latest types opened a terrific fire on us getting one hit forward and wounding two of a crew of six pounder gun crew lying on the deck. She closed in on us at 400 yard range, the action bell sounded and things were lively for a time. Our foremast gun got in a hit in the fourth round. Our other gun recorded several hits. Having been firing salvos for 10 minutes she rolled over and sank. This was a lovely scrap and our fourth bag.

"Our next engagement was a few days later 15 miles N W. of Trevose Head, but being mixed up with other patrols she disappeared on the arrival of an armed trawler.

"Our little ship had marvellous luck in her Royal Naval career as a decoy ship being dismasted in February 1917, rescued from a heavy N.W. gale 10 miles off Ushant and towed into Brest. After the

Armistice she proceeded to Falmouth and on December 6 was opened for public exhibition and to boost War Bonds. On the first day £16,000 was received while the proceeds of the eight days amounted to £36,000.

"Now, her work done, the good old *Mary B. Mitchell* is back at her peaceful occupation. She is a great little ship and will always have a place in the recollections of those privileged and proud to serve in her."

June 30, 1990

Thanks to the *MBM*

FROM Mr. Bert Prior of Tresco-Place, Falmouth, comes an intriguing memory regarding the *MBM Q9* mystery ship *Mary B. Mitchell*.

He writes: "Complementing the recent contributions sent in by my friends Norman Bishop and Gordon Mann about the *Mary B. Mitchell*, I recall that while acting as decoy the *MBM* engaged in fishing while on station off the S.E. coast of Ireland. She came into Falmouth to replenish supplies about every two weeks at the same time landing her catch which was sometimes considerable.

"My father was Harold Prior who was a war-time crew member based at Falmouth, used to bring home some of this very mixed catch which was freely distributed, and after making her selection my mother would parcel the remainder and tell me to take it along to various friends.

"While in port the crew were accommodated in lodgings and one member stayed next door to where I lived in Norfolk Road.

"As a six or seven year old lad I had no problem getting into the naval base when I said I wanted to see my Dad and on one occasion meeting my next door neighbour there he took me on board the *MBM* which was berthed alongside a wharf.

"He lifted me from wharf to ship as the *MBM* was surging badly and showed me his bunk which he used when at sea.

"I was certainly acquainted with her exploits and believe it was fairly common knowledge among the local people at the time she was operational, such was the lack of security during WW1."

July 28, 1993

The World War 1 "Q" ship Mary B Mitchell *at the Prince of Wales pier, fund raising after the Great War. Later she returned to the coal trade*

Bombed and strafed by the Germans

The ever-increasing references these days to the Second World War have for one 88-year-old woman revived memories of those dramatic times, half a century ago, when Cornwall was very much in the front line.

Mrs Haywood, now living near Shaftesbury, formerly Mrs Elizabeth (Betty) Rogers of "Barnes Cottage", Grove Hill Road, Mawnan Smith, has particular reason to remember those days, for as a result of a bombing raid she lost the sight of one eye. Glass splinters caused the injury.

Mrs Rogers (then the wife of Lt. Col. W.E. Rogers) was in "Barnes Cottage" with her young son, Anthony, when a sea mine exploded nearby and destroyed the building.

On another occasion early in the war Mrs Rogers was out pushing her son in his pram above Grebe beach when a German fighter, flying from West to East, strafed the beach. Fortunately no-one was injured.

Mrs Hayward said it was believed the Germans had a training airfield in Brittany where bomber pilots were instructed. They came nightly over Cornwall and dropped bombs wherever they saw a light. On one occasion a stick of bombs fell off the road to Treworval. Three exploded causing no damage. One remained, and a bomb disposal unit came and loaded it on to their lorry. P.C. Pascoe in the village had recently installed a plate glass window in his shop and was so delighted it remained intact that he gave the bomb disposal crew £10. Hardly had he done so than the bomb blew up—destroying both the lorry and the window!

A girls' school from London was evacuated to the village, and the girls found homes there. Most settled in happily, but two girls who had no local links were sent home. The night after they left, the bungalow to which they had been allocated received a direct hit and the owners were killed. This was caused by one of two sea mines intended for Falmouth Bay, but a strong Easterly wind was blowing and the mines drifted farther over the land. The one that destroyed the bungalow also took the roof off Carwinion House. The other landed in the garden of "Loenter" which was totally destroyed. By a miracle the owners and two evacuees were unhurt. "Barnes Cottage" was also destroyed at this time. Mrs Rogers recalls "The front of the Gundrys' house, just up the road, fell away. It looked like a dolls' house with all the rooms exposed."

Then there was the great invasion scare. A leaflet was sent to everyone telling them what to do "if the invader comes". We were to evacuate our homes and take with us a case containing necessities. A great talking point was what to put in one's "invasion case"!

The Fox family invited a great many people to take refuge in their Cider House (on the way to the beach at Glendurgan). This was a very ancient building, half underground, and built into the side of the hill. Luckily the invaders never came.

Mrs Haywood recalls that during the war the only shops in Mawnan were the P.O. (business only), a small butcher's shop and P.C. Pascoe's store, selling a few groceries and general goods (this was where Plater's is now). By the shop was P.C. Pascoe's bowling green, a strip of immaculate green velvet sward—the pride and joy of P.C. Pascoe. Once a week Lloyds Bank opened for an hour or so, bread was brought up from Constantine by Mr Belbin, and a butcher's van also called.

January 1994

Bomb disposal squad loading a UXB into lorry

Young evacuees afraid to walk in the woods

In every community there are public figures who because of their work become familiar to the majority of people. They may be school teachers, members of the medical profession, police, fire officers or clergymen.

Thus, on a recent visit to Mylor I sought the location of the home of Mrs Eileen Prout, everyone I asked immediately answered: "Oh, you want Nurse Prout...!" This lively 80-plus-year-old lady who many years ago retired from the nursing profession, was District Nurse in the Mylor district for a number of years. As such she will always be remembered.

She was born in Redruth and trained as a nurse with the Devon and Cornwall Nursing Association at Durnford Street, Plymouth.

It was while in training that she met her husband-to-be, Mr Rodney Prout, then a radiographer in the Royal Navy.

The couple were married in Mylor Church in 1938. They have one daughter, Miss Susan Prout of Mylor, a BT employee, and incidentally, a Celtic dance team member.

After the war, on completion of 14 years in the Navy, Mr Prout came out of the service and took over his father's business of a car hire and petrol filling station in Mylor. He ran this business until he retired in the 1970s. Mr. Prout died in 1992.

Earlier Mrs Prout had been a midwife in the Chesterfield Nursing Home, Bristol and a district nurse at Ludgvan, then just before the war, took over these duties from Nurse Boswell, in the Mylor district in 1939.

Her area included Flushing, Restronguet, Trefusis and to the bottom of Bissom Hill, outside Penryn.

At first she rode a bicycle, then purchased an Austin 7 for £35—"A marvellous little car which I had for all my nursing days, and which never let me down."

Whatever the weather the area had to be covered. She remembered going to Enys on one occasion and delivering a baby in one of the cottages by the lake there.

Then came the war—and the evacuees. Mrs Dorrien-Smith of Greatwood was the Red Cross Commandant and Mrs Prout a Red Cross worker. "We had to scrub out the Tremayne Hall (then the Church hall), and then the poor little evacuees came. It was a sad story. Four of them were sent to one of the cottages at Enys and they were afraid to walk in the woods in winter."

She remembered having a cottage in Lemon Hill to which many of her patients had to come. During an air raid early in the war, when she was going to see a patient at Carclew, bombs were dropped on Mylor, destroying four cottages in Lemon Hill and one in New Row. A number of people were killed.

To provide a better water supply with which to fight incendiary bombs, a stream from Enys was diverted into the creek stream.

For nearly 20 years she has been Leader of the Mylor Darby and Joan Club, but her major hobby for many years has been wood carving. A Mrs Metcalf came to live in Mylor. She was a skilled wood carver and Falmouth Technical College asked her if she would run a class. She agreed, and Mrs Prout used to transport her by car to and from classes. As a result she watched the pupils at work, was persuaded by Mrs Metcalf to try her hand and speedily became interested. In her home she has many fine examples of her skill, ranging from fruit bowls (one in Yew, made from part of a tree which blew down in Perran ar Worthal churchyard, and which has been exhibited in America) to a seies of "mother and offspring"' studies including a penguin and chick, fish and other animals and their young.

Not so long ago there was a ring at her front door bell. When she answered there stood a well-dressed man who asked for 'Nurse Prout'. "I was," she replied, "but that was long ago." "I'm ...." (he gave his name). It was one name she vividly remembered from evacuee days. As a youngster he had fallen in the creek and cut himself severely. Mrs Prout had had the job of staunching his wounds. She had never forgotten the incident, and he too had never forgotten her, and nearly 50 years later had called to see her and thank her for her efforts then.

Mrs Prout has one lasting memory of D-Day. A nursing sister friend and she, in Bristol, had June 6 1944 as a day off, and were taking tea in the garden when they saw a never-ending procession of aircraft flying overhead. The decided "something was on". How right they were!

February 1994

Famous visitors

In both the Great War (1914-18) as well as the Second World War (1939-1945) Falmouth played a key role because of its geographical position. Many famous personalities entered the port including members of European royal families in the latter conflict. According to a book entitled "Unreliable Witness" by Nigel West, published in 1984, Admiral Wilhelm Canaris who became head of the German Abwehr and was executed in Flossenburg concentration camp in April 1945 for complicity in the 20 July plot against Hitler, visited Falmouth in 1915. After his ship, the German cruiser *Dresden*, was scuttled in Chilean waters in April 1915, and the crew interned, Canaris escaped. With forged identity papers he trekked across the Andes to Buenos Aires where he boarded a steamer bound for neutral Holland via Falmouth. The port authorities at Falmouth were fooled by Canaris's faked documents and he continued his journey to Berlin where he reported for duty in October 1915.

Mata Hari the famous spy, whose real name, although she was Dutch, was Mrs Marguerite McLeod, was supposed to have worked for Canaris from Paris. She was arrested by the French on February 12, 1917 and shot at Vincennes after being found guilty of spying for the Germans.

Earlier, according to official stamps on her Dutch passport, in 1916 when trying to return to the Hague via Madrid from Paris she boarded the *SS Hollandia* at Vigo and was detained and questioned by British police officers at Falmouth. She was released, but instead of going on to Amsterdam she returned to Madrid.

The dancer, according to other records, was fulfilling a dancing engagement in Madrid when information reached England that she had been consorting with members of the German Secret Service and might be expected before long to be on her way back to Germany via Holland. This happened early in 1916. The ship put into Falmouth and she was brought ashore, together with her very large professional wardrobe, and escorted to London.

It is believed this happened on November 13, 1916. Whatever conflicting reports there may be about her movements there is no doubt that this famous, internationally-known and reportedly beautiful spy actually came to Falmouth.

February 1994

Lt Cdr Robert Hichens

Lt Cdr Robert Hichens, D.S.O. & Bar, D.S.C. & Two Bars, R.N.V.R., a solicitor practising in Falmouth in the 1930s, lived in Flushing and was married to a member of the Enys family of Enys. He was a man of considerable vigour and ability, a keen sailor and an able mechanic with an interest in motoring. He drove his Aston Martin three times in the Le Mans races, gaining the Rudge Whitworth Cup in 1937. As war became inevitable he urged the Lords of the Admiralty to form a Supplementary Force in support of the R.N.V.R. by signing up experienced Yachtsmen who were members of Yacht Clubs around Britain, yet were unable to spare time for training with the R.N.V.R. This was done and Hichens was called up with the R.N.S.R. after war broke out, but was refused entry into Coastal Command as at 29 he was considered too old, a decision which was refuted at a later date.

He was serving on a Fleet Sweeper at the time of the evacuation of Dunkirk, and was sent to help with the evacuation. He found many of the soldiers were having great difficulty in clambering into the various craft which were attempting to transfer them to larger ships waiting for them in deeper water. When his own ship had instructions to return to Dover, he begged permission to remain behind to assist in the last efforts of evacuation. Using his considerable powers of organisation and leadership, he did invaluable work embarking the exhausted men, and later received his first decoration in recognition of these efforts.

Robert Hichens

Later in the war he was posted to one of the newly formed Motor Gun Boat flotillas of Coastal Command. Their role was the protection of coastal shipping, the destruction of enemy E-Boats, and the harrassment of enemy convoys. Much of the fighting took place close to the enemy coast in range of enemy long-range guns and searchlights.

The M.G.B.s went out in small numbers, two, four or perhaps six boats prowling in the night, often wallowing in icy waters, engines cut to avoid detection as they waited for signs of the enemy. When the enemy appeared they attacked with all the fury of angry wasps. This type of warfare was the modern equivalent of the hand-to-hand fighting of naval actions of bygone years, direct and dangerous contact with the enemy; the type of warfare that would have suited Edward Pellew and certainly Hichens. It required accuracy, daring and brilliant leadership; a second's indecision could mean swift death.

As a commander of these boats Hichens was supreme, and his name became a legend in Coastal Command, and most of the tactical theory of motor gunboats was developed and practised by him. His loss in action was a severe blow to Coastal Command

In Falmouth today, young boys and girls undergo training for the Navy at a Shore Training Ship named *T.S. Robert Hichens* in memory of this remarkable man.

(The above has been taken from Lady V.M. Redwood's book "Trefusis Territory" which includes the history of Flushing.)